To Beverly
Enjoy!

June 2019

THE SYCAMORE SEED

(2nd Edition)

THE SYCAMORE SEED

(Poems 1980-2012)

J.D. Mallinson

To order additional copies of this book, contact:
Xlibris Corporation
1-888-795-4274
www.Xlibris.com
Orders@Xlibris.com
70589

CATEGORIES	Page
Nature	9
People And Places	83
The Arts	169
Miscellany	239
History	285
Appendix	359

PUBLICATION RECORD

BOOKS

Spirit of Place	Envoi Poets Publications, 1990
By Northwest	National Poetry Foundation, 1991
Composition of a European City	University of Salzburg Press, 1996
Evidence of Time	University of Salzburg Press, 1997

ANTHOLOGY CREDITS

Poet's England 18, Lancashire	Headland Publications, Liverpool
Poet's England 20, Cheshire	*do.*
Envoi Summer Anthology 1990	Envoi Poets Publications, Dyfed, Wales
Home Thoughts	BBC Publications, London
Summoning the Sea	University of Salzburg Press
(Festschrift for Professor Hogg)	
Tales for the Trail	Birch Brook Press, Delhi, NY
Birdsong	Seren Books, Bridgend, Wales
Versatility	Tears in the Fence, Dorset UK
Men in the Company of Women	Edgar & Lenore's Publishing House, Sherman Oaks, CA.

JOURNAL CREDITS

Contemporary Review, Cencrastus (*Scotland*),
English (*Journal of the English Association*),
Envoi, Episcopal News, The Frogmore Papers, The Good Society Review,
Journal of Contemporary Anglo-Scandinavian Poetry,
Kit-Kat Review (USA), The New Welsh Review, Ore,
Orbis International Poetry Quarterly, Outposts Poetry Quarterly,
The Poet's Voice (*Salzburg*), Poetry Nottingham, Prospice,
Psychopoetica (*University of Hull*), Stand Magazine, The Swansea Review
(*University of Swansea)* The Yorkshire Journal.

RADIO

Poems regularly featured on BBC Northwest *Write Now* series of poetry broadcasts.

AWARDS

Northwest Arts Publication Grant
Yeats Society (Oxford): Seal of Achievement
Scottish International Open Poetry Competition: Finalist
BBC Northwest *Home Thoughts* Competition: Runner-up

NATURE

Nature and Wisdom never are at strife
                                      Plutarch

HARMONIES

Waves of field sparrows
flood the lake's green edge,
the marshy shallows.

In sudden fright they rise
into the dense cascade
of leaves, their ardent song

unconscious of its depths,
its hidden springs. Like that
unconscious stealing up on oneself

of a sense of harmony
within the natural world:
how trees bend to the wind;

how the wind ignites the trees.
Water lapping gently under eaves
is the enigma of birds singing:

we hear what they feel;
but they remain deaf to
our voiced misunderstandings.

NEWBORN FOAL

He lies in the leaning meadow,
sad-eyed among buttercups,
wondering what can be made
of his unexpected existence.

The morning air smells green,
the fresh green of early spring;
boughs thickening with leaves
map the high, enigmatic sky.

The mare has no firm answers;
she strolls to the field's edge,
gazes wistfully down the lane
forging dreamily ahead.

The foal, now aware of distance,
flexes untested, rubber legs
and fumbles to his mother's side;
but not into the inside of her mind.

SHAG ON THE FARNE ISLANDS

Black, they keep their somber watch
on giant slabs of pillared rock,
lashed by waves to the wind's mast.

Or string in thin black line
tethered to a hanging sky,
awaiting news from the ocean east:

something to convey a meaning
to the long, unspoken years
on their island outpost in the bay.

When nothing comes, they go in search,
combing the contours of the sea,
rhythmically beating widow-wings

in the silence of the deep-bereaved;
where echoes on wave-deafened rocks
the plaintive cry of kittiwakes.

THE SYCAMORE SEED

This voyager trims his sail,
spins from the leaf's anchorage
on a voyage of pure discovery,
finding what it means to be
the embarkation of a tree.

All is now possible, or nothing:
the seed sows the argosy
of the high-blown sycamore
probing the atmosphere;
or it is stillborn, becalmed.

As it is with the seed of man,
winged as thought itself:
endless potential devolves
from one frail actuality,
from an embryonic plan.

The whole growing universe
might be one flowing thought,
a unique seed sown
inside a universal mind,
germinating throughout time.

CATKINS

They strew the ground
like fat caterpillars,
or furry slugs,
or evicted snails;

mute, impassive,
waiting for the action
to grip them from below,
drawing them down

into the womb of life
at the birth of poplars.
Or they litter the sidewalk,
to be crushed underfoot,

the seed translated
to that stony ground
that does not bear fruit,
piling one stone upon another;

not in the vital forms
of the *Sagrada Familia,*
but in the gaping shapes
of concrete cityscapes.

(The *Sagrada Familia* is the Barcelona cathedral
begun by Antoni Gaudi in 1883 and scheduled to
be completed in 2026)

CANADA GEESE

Saint David's Day.
Two pairs return
from annual migration
to this disused canal
they unfailingly locate
from navigation aids
viewed aerially.

Spring rains have swelled
the static water-level,
to swim the crowns
of windswept, blanched,
repeated weeds.
Strong westerlies
form rolling waves

they ply against,
oblivious of traffic
on adjacent motorways;
of railroad freight,
commuter trains,
the bustling city
just a day-return away.

This idling water
represents a wilderness
to them, its untrod bank
a fine environment
to nest in and to breed;
double their number
should arrive next spring.

REED WARBLER

Clinging to cattails
at the edge of the lake,
the male holds forth
his courtship song of
astonishing vocal range.

A receptive female
audits the performance:
in choosing a mate,
she intuitively responds
to the vocalist's take.

Lured initially by
the purity of his music,
she may also sense
a comparable facility
at practical skills,

like building a nest
and foraging for food.
Once courting is over
and breeding begins
in the whispering reeds,

from being a perky
airborne troubadour,
he reverts his song
to a less enchanting,
more pedestrian theme.

THE DAWN CHORUS

The tiny sedge warbler
commands a vocal range
of fifty-plus notes;
a most prolific and
versatile composer,
he never sings the same
song twice over.

He's just one member
of the morning chorus.
By vocal intercourse,
birds learn if kin survived
the predatory night,
and their precise location
in the woodland station.

When spring arrives,
the choir is swollen
by those returning daily
from far-flung places,
clearing oceans, deserts,
man-made hazards,
mountain ranges.

All draw at varying pitch
on seemingly endless
impromptu repertoires,
improvising freely,
in an ecstasy of feeling,
often beyond the scope
of merely human hearing.

EUCLID IN THE PARK

I like to sit awhile amid
the pale, the sapling April sun,
on a simple wooden bench
inside the geometry of floral beds.

And contemplate the gentler use
of public funds not spent on war
and its disquieting rumors,
but on frail, unfratricidal plants.

A clump of daffodils stands
despoiled by dogs; or by vandals
avenging life's lost chances
on the blameless stalks.

Roses well cut back in concave plots
dangle Latin names on metal tags,
filling out a Flora of a kind,
adding to the humus of the mind.

Parallelogram of gravel paths
breeds in damper spots a hardy moss
that freely multiplies beneath
parabolic boughs of horse chestnut.

LARCH

At the first stirring of spring,
it looks about as lifeless
as a spent Christmas tree,
its brittle boughs clutching
clumps of rusting leaves.

New shoots soon appear,
like tips of paintbrushes
a colorist might dip,
almost absent-mindedly,
into the paler greens.

Other conifers preen
and glisten in the April rain,
sharpening their needles
in readiness for summer's
stiffer growing pains.

The larch, long sere,
denuded, winter-bound
in deep-frozen ground,
rouses from its torpor
to steal the woodland scene.

CROCUS SONNET

Gaze into the crocus depths,
amid the veils of folding flesh
of striate mauve descending
into deeply-chaliced heliotrope.

Thus unsung, recondite world
is lit by vivid stamen lights;
alight, the inner lamp-like globe
burns with an amber glow.

The still perfection of its form
lies here, undisturbed by bees;
its season spanning hours or days
is shattered by one fickle storm,

its petals past, stem bent,
allure neutered, pollen spent.

BEE IN EARLY SPRING

He will not remit an instant
on his milking mission,
tacking in on sudden gusts
of the thin March wind,
to hang capsized upon
the budding currant bush.

He tries a new trapeze routine,
to tease the nectar
from these grudging cups;
they do not yield to sorties
of the raiding bees, only to
the sun's long probing tongue.

He quickly shifts his focus
to early-season blooms:
the crocus, at a pinch;
while daffodils and tulips,
indulging spring color,
vie with aspiring hyacinths.

A strong gust of wind
spins him out of kilter;
disoriented, flung high
across the sky, he re-aligns
his approach-flight warily
and, in the end, unerringly.

STICKLEBACKS

Mating of these minnows
is one of Mother Nature's
more ephemeral displays.

The male builds a nest
with weeds uprooted from
the bottom of the stream:

a ploy to lure a female
chancing nonchalantly by
to venture in to lay.

Next comes a shimmering,
quivering motion along
her taut silver flanks:

their sole romantic moment
before she darts away,
leaving him to guard

and tend the fertile eggs,
one eye on the kingfisher
alertly perched above.

No talk of love.

GARDEN IN MAY

Apple trees
in crimson flood
are deep in leaf
and clenching bud.

Spirea spreads
with careless grace
tapered fingers
draped in lace.

Potentilla held
in yellow thrall
grows profusely
by the old stone wall.

The lawn smooths out
her rumpled smock,
decked in daisy,
dandelion and dock.

Tulips sway
beneath the sill,
raise torn flags
for fading daffodil.

CARROUSEL

Hard on the late spring,
the garden grows apace;
starters in the race for life
run till the weeds exceed
the careful cultivation.

Creatures with a taste for greens
latch unprejudiced on leaves;
they unerringly target
the most succulent parts,
till all but the stalks is gone.

One life feeds freely on another;
or is it that all life is one,
links in a single chain?
Merely the typical forms rotate,
as the seasons swing them round.

SWALLOW PERCHING

Serendipity, it seemed,
that it alighted here
on the low fence-post;
a splash of sudden color
on a twilight world.

Before it lifted off
in liquid motion,
spilling into wing;
a flash of blue and white
in flood of flight.

A joy to see it here
beside high stooks of corn,
not scything air;
as if the reaper's arm
suspended arc.

Or the village clock
beyond the churchyard
lightly stopped
within this arbitrary silence,
marking time with scant alarm.

SWALLOWS ALOFT

They don't much take
to formation flying;
unlike the mallards,
or starlings massing
in dark farewell clouds.

They might be Spitfires
or Stukas on a solo run,
using the neutral sky
for aerobatic exercises
ending in steep dives.

Even these mavericks
must stand in some secure
relation to each other;
say, by built-in radar,
or avian telepathy

imposing on apparent
anarchy a subtle pattern
that meets collective needs
of swallows, however
these might be defined.

SWIFTS

Mercurial,
the species *aeronautes*
dart into encroaching dusk,
skim moonlit rivers,
flee tall trees,
buildings and all
material entanglement
in perpetual, restless,
silent exodus.

Pursuing insects,
looping, weaving,
sleeping on the wing
in unshaded air-lanes,
unlined avenues of sky,
they easily deceive
the merely human eye;
no wherefore or why,
they just fly.

CROWS

Confirmed individualists,
they allow themselves
ample room to maneuver.

Flying at a clear distance
from a notional centre,
no solo style is cramped.

They overshoot each other,
landing hectares apart
even when ostensibly

crossing open land together.
Meetings are kept brief:
they strut around for a while

shifting weight from their minds
like well-primed counsel;
even then displaying

a patent restlessness
to have done with the case,
threatening to take off

on singular expeditions.
Not much time for play,
unlike their magpie cousins

that probe the hinterland
between work and rest
to admirable effect.

MAGPIES ROUND THE HOUSE

They seem much intrigued
by my squat Scots pine,
retrieving fallen cones
to winkle out the seeds.

Or they dart up its trunk
to strip off bits of bark,
not for interlarding nests,
more as a playful lark.

Next comes a frolicsome
avian form of leap-frog;
followed by cartwheels,
somersaults, Scots reels.

Beaks probe into things
in routine curiosity,
until they come against
the totally unexplained.

Like four brick walls
looming up before them,
curiously unscalable,
the bipeds in them caged.

CRESTED PLOVER

Hard to distinguish
in the middle distance
from the magpie,
to the greener eye;
until, that is, it flies.

Then it will spread
its vaster span of wings
and lift into the sky.
How it loves to fly,
soaring over farmers' fields

and open heath,
from some vestigial fear
keeping well clear
of human habitations;
always in close touch

with its own colony.
Silent and alert,
it is easily overlooked
stalking the stubble
like a well-trained decoy.

Airborne, in chorus,
it brings the sky alive
with its thin, plaintive cry
too soon given
to the coveting wind.

HOUSE FINCH

A frequent caller
at the dawning garden,
fresh fruit-blossom
is a powerful draw,
its scent redolent
of ripe apples;
insects dug well in
over the long winter,
for want of tar oil,
are another focus
of his ceaseless trawl.

He ignores the crumbs
cast along the path
as chaff for sparrows;
blackbirds take them,
and the diehard magpie
when they catch his eye;
Sated, away he flies,
this tinted patrician
of suburban skies;
lest the rampant hawk,
menacingly, drops by.

THE RAIN ON THE SEA

The waves draw ever upwards,
in heavy curtains blacking out
the midday sun. A rain-curtain

is the whole world descending
on itself, immersing and
slaking itself, insatiably.

The sea is a bottomless well
that wells up to drink
and replenish itself.

A pelican pecking the life-blood
from her breast to feed her young
is like the sea and the rain.

And the rain on the sea
is wetness consoling itself
in a flood of implacable tears.

WRASSE

Some species operate
what is best described
as a bespoke grooming service,
setting up a chain of stations
at intervals across the reef,
to pick fish clean of parasites.

Quality of service varies
with the status of the client:
mean, high-profile predators
get meticulous attention;
short-changing them implies
the wrasse is swallowed live.

Next in rank come fish
with a broad oceanic range
that gives them greater scope
and say in grooming stations.
Wrasse cater to their needs
ahead of local coasters who,

at peak boutique times,
must wait patiently in line
and offer no complaint, even
when the cleaner cheats them
by nibbling bits of tissue
from lips and pectoral fins.

SPERM WHALES

They fall fast asleep
vertical amid the deeps,
their limp, massive frames
rocked by gentle eddies.

This cool water-bed
smoothly adapts itself
to their giant contours,
cradling and caressing them.

No cramp or stiff neck
as, deep-down refreshed,
they dive a nautical mile
in pursuit of live prey

devoured in quantities
that surpass the combined
trawl of the world's
commercial fishing fleets.

Confronting a giant squid,
they at length resurface
bearing scars of epic battles
in the arenas of the sea.

AT OCEAN'S EDGE

The tide rises slowly,
stringing mollusk beads
across lingering sands;
winnowing evenly,
mingling braids of weed
torn from the sea's wet hair.

A lightness of touch
holds the smallest infant
in its swirling embrace,
in the gentlest caress;
its reach of the beach
encapsulates happiness.

It conceals its retreat
in imperceptible steps
delicate as a child's,
yet well beyond innocence;
to its evergreen mystery
and bathysphere depths.

SEA CANVAS

The sun on the sea
is a Monet painting touched
by brushless strokes of light.

It is light turning liquid
over the broad expanse
of the sea's pigmented surface.

Endless impression of cobalt sky,
fusion of dream and the naked eye;
perfect transparency.

It is an unframed, unlimited
reproduction of itself,
outselling the pale imitations.

BREAKERS AT OGUNQUIT

Sweeping across the shore
with a dull, insistent roar,
their sound is ever the same,
yet well beyond monotony.

Clad in mini-bikinis,
sun-kissed nubile nereids,
salt sea spraying hair,
rush to their cool embrace,

wading the lacy shallows,
surfing the crests of waves.
When the long tide slides out,
draining the sunlit bay

to await its patient return,
it will usher identical waves,
with the same insistent roar
as those that hit these sands

millions of years ago.
Or is each breaker unique,
a one-off, unrepeatable feat,
over the moment it peaks?

RESONANCES

White pebble on the beach,
washed smooth by the sea,
might pass for a gemstone;
not fired and honed deep
in the bones of the earth,
but cut by wind and wave.

Now in heavy bud the rose
shall one day soon outshine
the ruby and the sapphire,
if for a briefer time; as on
the heath is heard less long
the song of nightingales.

These pure modes of being,
of themselves complete,
are different from our own,
distinct; their inner life
(so snared are we by surfaces)
unfolds in pristine mystery.

THE SECRET DRINKER

He dropped into a nearby copse
to slake an ancient thirst,
drinking in trees that stood
on supple plinths and played
into the basin of the sky.

Rippling trees were not unlike
stately fountains wildly playing,
endlessly spraying leaves
of Lincoln green, clear as pools,
deep as undulating England.

Their pure liquidity became
so much deposit in the bank
compounding daily to itself,
without the ritual paying in,
the agony of drawing out.

He stood in debt to no one,
here within a wealth of wood;
no teller noted which amount,
he could freely draw forever
on his growing green account.

SILVER BIRCH

Its smooth bark gleams
in bright sunlight lighting
its milky way to other stars.

It tapers swaying through
its whole bole-length,
rippling in the liquid air,

parting invisibly where
spindle branches weave
a filigree of tissue-leaves.

Rent by a sudden breeze,
it trembles from its canopy
down to the deeper roots,

dark sutures of the soil
winding it and binding it
between two living spheres.

WEEPING WILLOW

The trunk tilts forward
forty-five degrees,
like some Tower of Pisa
of the arboreal world,
challenging gravity.

It casts all boughs
before it, finely tapered,
as a shapely maiden
on a market stall leans
forward with her wares.

Cleavage is between
the boughs as they divide,
spill, shoot, distill;
the tears it sheds fall
thickly to the ground.

Standing underneath it
on a rainy summer's day
will land one in the shower;
no controls are needed,
it self-adjusts the spray.

JUNE EVENING

Sun casts lengthening shadows,
extending oaks and poplars
across the verdant acres
of summer playing fields.

Boys assemble cricket stumps
against the boundary wall;
lean into a leaner stroke,
bat against a seamless ball.

In this lantern evening
time hangs magically longer,
spinning out the loom of youth,
our zest for living stronger

for its having no recall.
Past and future time defer
to one eternal present where
our childhood dreams recur.

RED ADMIRAL

One may watch it hovering
in the depths of summer,
towards late-evening
when heat is heaviest,
draining the lanes of air.

Long-suspended
in a spiral of torpidity,
it beats tissue-wings
in a bid to break out,
to escape the limp humidity.

Becalmed, as in
sea of a high salinity,
it keeps feebly abreast
of the ocean-evening
conjuring, coaxing breeze;

affording us the time,
the occasion to admire
this nautical high-flier,
the most resplendent
of British butterflies.

CANALS

They do not flow like rivers,
fill like lakes and overspill;
still, these captive waters live
on different levels governed
not by nature but by locks.

They shape the narrow boats
adrift along the inland coasts,
beguiling crew with shifting scenes,
the things that live and breathe
beside these static streams.

People living out their dream
of freedom remain captive
in their tideless ebb and flow;
beyond their narrow gate canals
have nowhere in this world to go.

DISUSED CANAL BASIN

It extends from the gates
of a long-abandoned lock
to an old stone bridge
ferrying the railroad
that has overtaken it.

Neglected, it idles here,
a timeless backwater
serving no purpose worthy
of an upkeep, a dredging,
a clearing of the weeds.

Unused, yet not useless
to the shoals of roach
broaching wider water
to take what tempting bait
the children improvise.

Nor to the geese that ply
these slow, wasting fens
in a single fluid line
under the gander's eye;
nor to timid water hens.

Ponies randomly appear,
gaze bemused into the pool
where exposed tree-roots,
tenacious as embedded stone,
twist in a dry antiquity.

DAMSEL FLIES

Skimming the canal,
well clear of the reeds,
they maintain a thin line
just this side of survival.

Advanced aeronautics
in the midsummer noon
spin out in blue rings
on a confident breeze.

Innocent as Icarus,
one ventures too close;
the deceptive waters
close in on its wings.

It bobs on the surface,
rocked by strong ripples
it lived with in harmony
till the other reneged.

Rescue crew arrive;
they hover above it,
combining workmanlike
to winch it up live.

They too are overcome;
in a flurry of spent wings
they swirl in the eddies,
wasted as leaves.

HORNETS

Holes are just large enough
to permit their free escape
from earth's glazed atmosphere;
each has its allotted place
in the dark, humming labyrinth.

In intense heat of high summer,
the clay soil is caked, sun-baked;
the noon nest becomes a furnace
they soon abandon for the cooler
welcomes of the circling air.

A giant beech stands by,
inviting to its depths of green;
the hornets emerging one by one
sample the cool cross-currents
beneath a parasol of leaves.

They bob and weave freely,
diving through the liquid breeze
that is the hornets' bathing pool
soothing the fierce, striped body heat,
disarming them of instant sting.

TERMITES

They ably assemble
elaborate earthen constructs,
with ventilation ducts
to maintain a constant
internal temperature
when the prairie burns
around them like a furnace.

Each insect has its own
specialized role as soldier,
forager, skilled worker
undertaking key repairs;
aristocrats are the dainty,
airborne, mating alates
serving future generations.

They defend their walls
against ants, aardvarks, rains
that wash the earth away;
all in thrall to the queen,
an egg-laying machine
controlling the process
with subtle signal-scents.

GNATS AMONG PINE-TREES

They dance weightless,
barely observable,
in the pines' deep shade.

Year on year,
barely discernably,
the pines increase in girth.

They seem oblivious
of all this frenzied,
siesta-time activity.

What does it portend,
this fandango of gnats,
for the cycles of earth?

Do they visit plants
to aid in pollination?
Are their gyrations

addressed to themselves,
like a ballet troupe
in closed rehearsal?

Until they fall and add,
after a frantic life-span,
brief humus to the soil.

SURPRISE PARTY

The last day
of the praying mantis
is in some ways
a kind of celebration.

Only problem,
the glut of food:
everything, *everyone*
is edible.

Soon there are
too many gate-crashers,
ants formicating
all over the place.

The hostess,
quite overwhelmed,
gets carried out
limb by limb.

                    *

I like those ants
that are nectar farmers;
or leaf-cutters
husbanding trees.

Those that patrol
the forest floor
in aid of bio-diversity,
objectively scattering seeds.

GARDEN SPIDER

You create your own space
out there, enclosing a tad
of the great outdoors
in a silken web that bends
the sun's taut morning rays
in captive beads of dew;
and you, moving slowly
towards the centre of things,
sit there in radial light
to await an outcome.

On sudden impulse,
you invade our space,
the dim halls of mankind.
They are unkind. Soon lost
on the wilderness parquet floor,
you flee this way and that
the infinite surface madness
which shows no landmarks,
no bearings bearing you
back to your throne.

SLUG

He must slowly sense
the most opportune time,
in lame humidity after rain,
to emerge from his cranny
beneath stones and rotting logs.

He browses even more slowly,
in conspicuous consumption
across measureless lawns
and the vegetable plot,
deftly picking his greens.

What is one confident stride
to a man walking his dog,
imbibing the thriving air,
may be many miles to a slug
lugging his silvery tail.

He does not count the hours
spent on his labored journey
as so much interval lost;
no more than he questions
his much vaguer destination.

MICROBES

It was naively thought
that bugs could be scuppered
by well-targeted drugs.

Antibiotic means anti-life;
but bugs are revealing
depths of resilience.

They do not know in advance
what the army of whitecoats
will throw at them next.

More like secret Maquis
than front-line troops,
they invent novel defenses,

reinforcing cell walls
against chemical invaders;
mounting counter-attacks;

assuming new guises
from genetic mutations;
they're full of surprises.

There are tactical strategies
at the microbial level,
primitive, yet hardly simple.

They respond to onslaughts
with swiftness and cunning;
superbugs are up and running.

TREES APPROACHING WINTER

All Saints Day.
In borough parks,
on sidewalks through the town,
they have broken cover
to run full course
their leafless marathon.

To reveal,
in this annual remission,
the gist of their philosophy:
working upwards
from firm principles
rooted in the soil.

There are vital links
with folk cultures
promoting languished crafts
that have survived
the industrial age,
the canopy of the past.

A sturdy trunk
supports the sinuous limbs
grown increasingly
tenuous and refined,
like processes of thought,
fertility of mind.

BIRDS OF PASSAGE

Wings in steady rhythmic
progress over downward
depths of current stroke
in one extended motion
the pendant breasts of air.

Prow into the wave-burst
of the clouds, they keep
a close-knit V-formation
on the long migration
to the prisms of the south.

One stalls and dips,
brinked back by some
subconscious focus
not to let him falter falling
through unanchored sky.

Towards the far horizon
their numbers start to swell
from several directions;
starlings they must be,
massing over open sea.

DEATH OF A MAGPIE

His flight-path ended
here upon the moss;
talons lying crippled
by his flanks no longer
strut him proudly
through tall grass,
nor fasten on what takes
his chancing eye.

Feathers quiver
in the arrowed wind,
that hovered like
a broad and jagged kite
lofting over copse
and river vale;
or beat like battling
helicopter blades.

Head laid back in
deeper flights of sleep
still thrusts the sharp
stiletto of his beak;
his torso measured by
a dark-green bottle fly
that stalks his weary breast
and beaten heart.

BIRD-WATCHING IN WALES

At last extent of Pembrokeshire
a clinging path holds its breath
against the lip of sheer cliffs
shoring up Saint David's Head;
in gorse and densely-matted beds
stonechat linger, linnets spin.

A half-island's subtropic walk
descends from Penmaen Burrows
to bays lapping South Gower;
sea air lures the yellowhammer,
hones the solo flight of crows,
draws the dunnet to the hedge.

Climbing into depths of sky
above the high, lonely valleys
of the Cambrian mountains—
by Mynnyd Eppynt—buzzards
and the fork-tailed kite
hover at a rending height.

On middle reaches of the Dee
down to Llangollen, dippers dip
and swallows dart beneath
stone arches of the bridge;
feinting too against the drift
wagtail perches, lightly lifts.

BARN OWL

His white, sad face
is like a clown's grease-painted,
a clown hiding from us
behind nocturnal habitats.

Alert, impassive,
only sharp eyes move
inside the pale face-mask,
which rarely slips.

Eye feathers are antennae
conducting the slightest sound
around the round owl head
to hungry, pricking ears.

Like a specter he flits
across the wetness of the fens,
visiting death to small mammals
unalive to his presence.

MAPLES

Greetings come each season
from our lofty maple trees,
providing healthy, year-round
outdoor occupation.

First they strew the drive
with husks encasing leaf-buds;
winged seeds then quickly spin
in thousands to the ground.

Summer storms in violence
shower the sodden earth
with windfall twigs and sprigs
for kindling winter hearths.

Songbirds of varied pitch
seek out the higher boughs,
harmonizing blithely,
drenching us with sound.

Fall brings heavy labor
clearing spent, sere leaves
carpeting lawns and pavements,
clogging up the eaves.

In winter they maintain
a kind of tactful silence,
seeing our burden switch
to shifting heaps of snow.

The welcome shade they gave
all summer long is gone;
nor would they really wish
to screen the winter sun.

SUBURBAN PARK IN NOVEMBER

One might ideally need
the palette of Van Gogh
to paint the fiery maples.

Beeches' broad canopies
drift steadily away
to a lingering rusty haze.

Yellow-gold, the sunlit
domes of sycamores
in this fenced outdoors.

Silver birches, circumspect,
seem much less sure
of the season's purpose;

here is a reluctance,
an uneasy flickering,
a staggered withering,

no two leaves the same.
Still green, the northern oak's
just starting now to fade.

COPPER BEECH

It may sometimes seem
as green as any beech,
a deeper, burnished green
beneath its spreading shade;
with boles resembling
mildewed pillars,
solid, smoothly pale.

A deep sea-green:
bird-fish flitting through
its swaying fronds
have calls the mermaids
do not answer to,
and beds in which to lay
their mollusk eggs.

Some pigment on
the underside of leaves,
a given distance,
aid the trick of light;
it changes like the surface
of the sea reflected in
the hollows of the waves.

The world is rarely how it is,
more how it seems.

PRUNING THE HEDGE

This thorn hedge
struck by the woodman's axe
bares bunched knuckles,
as if fighting back.

Limbs split at parturition
from the fecund earth
lock in internecine strife
along the settled borders

of the stream
draining the braes
that grazed the herd
the hedge held back.

Laid back, too,
the hosts that thrived
in the knit economy
of hedgerows;

that cede to the steel plow,
demand for land unbalancing
the taut ecologies of earth,
digging us up from fixed roots.

AUTUMN GALE

It tugs at the roots
of the meadow grass;

swims the lake
clean over its banks.

It leaves tall trees
tipping their masts;

chases the clouds
till they race madcap.

It rattles casements,
lifts doors off the latch;

sweeps the cobwebs
from the mind's morass.

With a deft side-flick,
it removes one's hat;

flings the lone crow
clear out of his path,

has him battling back.

CRANE FLIES
(*Daddy-long-legs*)

Free-skating on the window pane,
all at once they seem
to fasten there and freeze
inside the day's cold frame.

Frail limbs out-splayed
like arms of mute appeal,
they peer disjointed
through the glass at our
ingrown, hermetic world;
at fires that gleam and grin
but do not burn.

Antennae work ceaselessly
for hint of some warm message
through the bitter glass;
it could only be the wind
deceiving them.

Wings poise as steadied
helicopter blades
too atrophied to climb
the rude autumnal air.
Sliding down the runway glass,
they crumple in upon themselves
in brittle mass of wasted limbs;
their wings are ailerons
triggered by relentless winds.

WOLVES

Adept predators, they move,
when locally reintroduced,
to the apex of the food chain.

In packs they attack bears,
whose fangs, claws and fur
are found undigested in scat.

From woodland habitats,
coastal species have been spotted
swimming miles from land,

on some marine odyssey
to distant, wooded islands
in the blue unruled Pacific.

They augment a staple diet
of deer, elk and rodents
by a surprising acquired skill:

wading in spawning grounds
of shallow pools and gravel,
for the annual salmon kill.

SQUIRRELS

Their runs are clearer now;
few lingering leaves
impede headlong descents
or lateral transfers
from branch to branch
of birch and sycamore,
ash, tupelo, maple.

They soon access
the windfall harvest:
beechnuts and the glut
of plump, ripe acorns
where the northern oak,
clinging to sere leaves,
rustles in the fitful breeze.

They like the feel
of this more open road,
like truckers shipped
of a heavy load;
it gives a keener sense
of arboreal freedom,
garnering winter stores.

EXTENDED LEASE

A host of young magpies
crowd the swaying branches
of a wayside evergreen.

The overspill string out
along a nearby street-lamp's
artificial bough,

which curves gently upward
out of the horizontal,
sere and unleafing;

like a modern annexe
to a listed building
or a period house.

None of the simple,
traditional home comforts;
just a bare concrete floor.

The magpies, unruffled,
take this in their stride;
they like to extemporize.

At dusk, when mandarin lamps
give sudden ersatz light,
they switch to curtained flight.

THE BADGER OF KEW GARDENS

Had he dined on ptarmigan,
on partridge or on quail,
no one might have minded;
even if mildly surmising
some humbler field fare
was more suited to his state.

But badger was a creature
of some gastronomic flair,
whose appetite took wings
among rare types of birds,
herons, avocets, flamingoes
gracing the gardens there.

Back along the earthworks
he raised in his defense,
they found him surrounded
by incriminating evidence,
his dim galleries lined
with clean-picked specimens.

Before these twilit dinners
were begun, this poacher
added just another touch
of pure, romantic elegance,
suggesting in the mind of badgers
a certain wry munificence.

In deep recesses of his lair
were bunches of wild bluebells
picked that day amid the tares.
Did he give them to his mate
before inviting her to dine
on this epicurean fare?

CHIPMUNKS

Rather unexpected,
disquieting even,
to see you in mid-winter
out busily foraging;
or under sparse canopies
darting from lair to lair
with rare impunity.

Is it from the Pacific
that this agnostic
Lenten license comes?
A maverick ocean current,
lightly dubbed El Nino,
that disturbs your sleep
across winter's peak?

Are you a harbinger,
in all innocence,
of dire events ahead:
shifting global drifts
you may be unaware of
at a conscious level,
yet sense in the blood?

That gull you into truancy
from time-honored modes
of pure rodent being;
as we too are gulled,
by established habits
and vested interests,
into burning fossil fuels.

LAKE IN WINTER

Fog, pierced by a shaft
of pale-yellow light,
curls back from the bank
to show layers of snow
slowly accumulating.

It reveals a crystal world
at the lake's arctic centre;
the still-life of birds
that summer thrives there,
migrants from another season.

Only quirky moorfowl stir,
picking their ginger way
across ice-floes banking
bitter reeds, their ousted home,
stiff and blanched as dried flax.

This is the survival world,
teeth of the earth's famine;
nothing green can now grow.
Ice world, ice kingdom,
its canopy is fog and snow.

BEECHWOOD

Boles and leafless boughs
writhe towards the sky,
questing, intending
the future shape of trees.

Mute sentinels
on the windswept hill,
they bear the brunt
of the storm's ill-will.

When they cannot bend
to its force, they yield,
their iron will contested,
hidden flaws exposed.

The dry beechnuts
littering the ground
in copious thousands,
to be crushed underfoot,

are discarded brittle shards,
the grist of windfalls
of the bounteous years
the rodent tooth gnaws.

SPARROW HAWK

Rhythmic beating of his wings
propels him, scythe-like,
over stubble fields invoking
all the cold reproach of winter.

Wings and tail-span fanning
inches over open ground
coordinate the ear and eye,
to plot the latent possibilities.

Soaring, he pirouettes on high,
like a ballet dancer poised
on the tip of motion, hovering
on the cusp of indecision.

Swiftly, a hidden score decides:
to rend the air in one thematic
dive; or to pitch into the vast,
the far-flung choruses of sky.

STALLION OUT TO GRASS

He stands stock-still,
long hours at a stretch,
to confront head-on
the relentless chill.

As if the concept of motion,
so vital in his prime,
were no longer relevant
to his prime leisure time.

Gazing stoically
at a deep-frozen world,
his breath climbs wraith-like
to the cloudless sky.

What sustains him
in this cheerless season,
if not sheer determination
to outface the cold?

Or fond dreams of spring,
of slowly strolling, grazing,
rolling over in fields
of dew-decked clover?

TIMBER RATTLER
(*Crotalus horridus horridus*)

At first bite of cold
he goes underground
to the ancestral home
restored each generation
since the colony took hold
a thousand years ago.

He adds one segment
to his cachet rattle
each complete year
he eludes the interest
of hawks, bobcats, foxes,
raccoons, eagles, men.

These colonial homes
widely honeycomb
the northern pinewoods
roamed by hardy hikers,
as by seasoned hunters
stalking white-tailed deer.

He reappears in spring,
heat-sensing his prey
before injecting it
with a hypodermic,
scanning the forest floor
for mice and small rodents.

LICHEN

Growing over tombstones
in the country churchyard,
it may be centuries old.

Airborne spores
lodge on the bare surface
defying wind, the stone's cold.

Not even violent storms,
gales, frost and snow
release its toe-hold.

Gentle rains help it
to attain its yearly goal:
accretion by a millimeter.

Until it blossoms orange,
gilding the perennial brows
of these inscribed menhirs;

imparting a kind of after-life,
a creeping immortality
to supine mortal bones.

URBAN SNOWSCAPE

Fresh snow falls on the town,
whitening and cloaking it,
bestowing a kind of unity
it does not normally possess,
drawing everything together,
eliminating separateness.

It is a bridal garment
that renews all things
to the purity of that point
in time we call Creation,
from which in all our
progress we digress.

A plume of foundry smoke
injects a sudden stain,
like the original stain
at the core of human life:
why we half love and,
half loving, are only half-alive.

ABANDONED QUARRY

They gouged and bled
the hillside here to build
their settled homes below
of pale, well-weathered
Yorkshire stone.

Spilled its cold entrails,
the rough-hewn boulders
long-exposed to moorland gales
eroding them, honing them
down to the barest bones.

Couch grass clings
to the chasm edge like
tufts of hair round some
slow-healing wound; moss
creeps into crevices in rock

to stage a come-back
in this scarred, pitted face
lodging the scant secretions
of the wind scoured from
the backs of millstone hills.

CHURCHYARD

Hard as iron it was,
and in this cold wood,
and in the pale interstices
between iron boles of trees,
fresh-turned mounds of earth
encrusted to a yellow rust;
in all this iron hand
plucked blossoms sprang
in scarlet ribbon of display.
No song-bird sang.

Hard-driven
by the arrowed wind,
the snow swirled over
old and fresh-filled earth
till all was one: the dead
and the un-quick lying
in one white winding shroud;
and drifted coldly over
stone and marble eaves.

PENGUINS

Ambling in single file
they climb inch by inch
the flank of a steep incline,
in the teeth of a biting gale.

Gaining the snow-plateau,
they huddle close together,
massing in thousands to hold
their hard-won ground;

sheltering their young
beneath dense feathers
to preserve their lives
at this threatening time.

When the storm has passed
and clearing skies recast
the ice in crystal sunlight,
they glide back to the sea,

never seeking to flee
the contours of their lives;
in this ultimate south,
snow-birding is out.

POLAR ICE

Tiny arctic fauna hibernate
inside it, well-insulated,
like igloo-dwelling Inuit.

It traps gas from the lake's
decaying vegetation, blooming
in ever more curious plants:

deep-frozen mushrooms
clinging to the under-surface,
lightly suspended in glass.

It transforms fallen twigs
and sprigs into frond-fossils
bedding in ice-meadows.

Ice-worms thrive inside it,
in the misty pockets of air,
slimming on shivering algae.

We have extended its reach
into ice-cream, iced drinks,
ice palaces, ice-rinks.

And the general ice-mare
of twenty-first century living,
built round the elegant ice-box.

PEOPLE AND PLACES

I wouldn't mind visiting China if I could get back the same day.
Philip Larkin (1922-85)

ST. ANDREWS

Little would the saint imagine,
trekking the stony roads
of Thrace and Asia Minor,
escaping in nick of time
from attempts on his life
before dying at Patras,
that his name would be borne
beyond the farthest outposts
of the Roman Empire.

Nor would he have guessed
that a small Scottish town
on the eastern seaboard,
a long shot from Hadrian's Wall,
would adopt his name,
honor it with a university
and become the spiritual home
of a famous eighteen holes,
the Mecca of modern golf.

Missionary activity of a sort:
endless legwork in pursuit
of lofted goals; the great
outdoors in all weathers;
a draw for devoted disciples
trailing the master round,
eager to embrace his lead,
hanging on each nuance, drift
and spin for moral uplift.

SOLWAY FIRTH

By Annandale we turn and take
the long, snaking road that breaks
through Dumfries into Galloway,
where hills arise steeped in pine,
slaking green the thirsting eye.

We leave behind majestic peaks,
crags, vales and wooded dales,
the lure of Wordsworth's Grasmere
and yonder land-locked lakes,
for the wildnesses of Solway.

And seek along the lonely strand
the play of wind and wave on sand,
shriek of tern, the gull's lay,
a dolphin breaking surface here
among the coves of Wigtown Bay.

Vikings here began their rout
after Cuthbert's monks fanned out
from remote, off-shore Iona,
on missions as far to the south
as St. Gallen and the northern alps.

YACHTS AT WINDERMERE
(*English Lake District*)

They rarely stay still,
even when their skippers,
marooned in offices and shops,
dream of a weekend spill.

Tied to colored buoys
in the shallows of the bay,
they spin around, gyrate,
as horn-piped sailors may.

Or bob their slender prows
into the heaving swell
from launches full of tourists
held in a scenic spell.

Theirs are lonely lives
between each Sunday sail,
the hatches battened down,
spare tackle tucked away.

When winter calls,
wreathing its heavy mists,
they perform, in sudden squalls,
fandangos on the lake.

DERWENTWATER
(*English Lake District*)

Lone yachtsmen glide
this broad, reflective water,
where wooded islands guide
the navigating eye in,
and stealing ever closer in,
to clear, unfolding views,
blue on a deeper blue;
a heron or a buzzard skews
towards the open sky.

Cumbrian Mountains rise,
fixed in immutability,
their dark, defensive centre
the locus of a mystery
sealed at the dawn of time:
a canticle in stone,
perpetually intoned,
as tumult of cumulus
drifts *sotto voce* by.

SILVERDALE
(Lancashire)

Coastal waders span
the mudflats stranded by
receding tides that hide
the shifting banks of sand.

Broad meadows flow
down to the shore, breaching
a containing wall in the lee
of overhanging trees, ivy

and knotted brambles'
stranglehold on pallid stone;
a greenish mist envelops all,
the silver-green of Silverdale.

On the green beach
no bathers hail; feckless sheep
drift out to graze along the wary
tidal way that weds the river

to the waves, where sirens
call the sea's return in
widows' weeds, from vessels
wrecked in Morecambe Bay.

RIBBLESDALE IN WINTER

The Ribble slowly flows
to join the lower Hodder,
beneath the riven clouds,
through low-lying meadows,
dank, depleted, sallow.

Sky is alive with crows
checking in from solo flights
to a round four dozen,
keeping in uneasy rows
some dark, listless coven.

Strung out in fallow fields
fringed with leafless beeches
patient in the vacant air,
they wait as we are waiting
for the seasons' slow turn.

Brief extempore forays
into the middle distance
fling them round the feudal hall,
its long, lingering past
veiled in mist, or rain-pall.

SADDLEWORTH
(Yorkshire/Lancashire border)

Bleak tracts of moorland
high above the habitation line
parcel into pastures formed
by crumbling dry-stone walls
opening at a broken stile.

Below, well-screened by trees,
modern redbrick homes
jostle with unnatural ease
the weathered stone of
weavers' three-tiered cottages.

Too sheer for hillside sheep
to climb, the valley's gaunt
and leaner side has no stone walls;
it balks all efforts to divide
the shadows of its seamless pall.

Angled on this Pennine rise,
a lonely tractor weaves a thread
among the folds of new-mown hay,
between the firmament of fields
and acres of the open sky.

MORRIS DANCERS AT SADDLEWORTH

Elaborate flower-pot hats
upon their craggy heads,
profuse in seasonal blooms,
are appropriate attire
for transcribing them
into the natural realm,
its spread of meadows,
woodland, rills and streams.

In dark knickerbockers
clasping at the knee,
striped waistcoats, hose,
any one of them could be
a spruced-up Worzel Gummidge
headed for a country ball
through fields and hedges
where late-summer stalls.

Belled clogs ring out
across firm open ground
sounding this robust,
medieval village dancing
to fiddle, drum, accordion.
Chauvinist male energy
and zest invest it,
boisterous, infectious.

MOORLAND INN

Settles on this northern wold
dusk that draws the fading light
down to the edge of darkness
over Diggle and the silent moors.

At hand, the weathered stone
of a gravemaker's former home
(the somber overtones persist)
rises dimly through the mist.

Cowering in the evening cold,
patrons flit like specters
in and out of softly-opened doors;
sip mulled ale 'neath sagging beams

unflagging on the flagstone floor,
a log fire roaring in the hearth.
Emerged, these shadows merge
with deeper shadows on the hill,

their lawful journey home arrested
by a peacock's sudden presence
behind them in the beech's lie;
chilling is its quasi-human cry.

HOLLINGWORTH LAKE

Swollen by brackish streams
coursing down the millstone hills,
it draws the moorhen and the mallard
sculling in among the reeds,
wild geese and stray gulls.

Calling too in wind and wave
the sail-club tucked into the bay
beside the sloping slipway,
where they wheel and wade
knee-deep at their aquatic trade.

Clarity of air redeems these hills,
and clarity of northern light,
to counterpoint the leaden weight
of sinking skies dissolving
into graying mist and acid rain.

Sky stoops to mirror-lake
to contemplate its drifting face;
it pales before the setting sun
beyond all time, beyond the moors,
their urgent space, towards the dream-like nebulae.

BY NORTHWEST

Tracts of wild moorland climb
above the steeples of the towns,
encroaching on the open sky.

They descend to stony valleys
carved by rushing streams that
drove the wheels of textile mills.

Bitten by hard circumstance,
lashed by the western gale,
a man disdains the minor ills;

concentrates on how to wrest,
within the patterns of decay,
a living from the living hills

that once enshrined -
industrious were their names -
prosperous cities of the plain.

HEPTONSTALL
(*West Yorkshire*)

It climbs the Pennines
by steep, cobbled streets
antique as the stark ruin
of its first parish church

erected in high sympathy
for St. Thomas Becket,
after his contract killing
by Henry 11's knights.

Several are its graveyards,
one for the forgotten dead
of long-gone centuries.
Sylvia Plath's remains

rest on the windswept face
of a stony, open hillside
scanning moorland sheep,
vicarage and village inn.

Old England here lives on
in its traditional civilities,
graced by the lack of pace
and grime of modern cities.

HOUSE FOR SALE

The windows were still
curtained in fine lace,
as on the day she changed them
pending her hoped-for return.

I approached the rear door,
half expecting mother's smile
greeting my day-long
homecoming from school.

No care-worn face
peered in apprehension at
the sound of footfalls broaching
this most intimate way in.

No television screen flickered
by the gas-misering fire;
all was closed, hard-closed
and bolted from within.

Only my own reflection
returned my stealing gaze
through the leaded window
where evenings she would sit

nursing fading memories
where fresh flowers grow,
acknowledging a half-known face
appeared above the hedge.

I twist the key in grudging lock,
stooping to gather the clutter
of uncorresponding mail
on my tentative way in;

pausing by half-open door
of the denuded living-room,
its empty hearth in fire-roaring,
family-assembling afterglow

down the deserted years
that bind the long-dead
with those whose voices rang
until barely hours ago.

THE ADVANCED STUDENT OF RUSSIAN
(Harold Fowweather)

Tuned to an old wireless
someone had moved
to a spare room at the library,
he searched in vain for living
words of spoken Russian.

He had never been there,
to this land of his fond imaginings,
but knew it like an exiled son
from the great books he had read
and compiled word-lists for
in notebooks, in black lead.

The task revived
his widowed hours,
gave grist to an aging mill;
daily he trudged on up the hill
to wage his lone campaign
on *War and Peace*, poring over
faded notes that emphasized
defeat across the blurred
and smudge-stained sheets.

Cold War stratagems
conspired against him:
hidden gremlins in the wireless box
jammed the broadcasts with static.
Golos Ameriki (Voice of America) was lost.

NEIGHBORS

This timeless couple leave
the house by the back door
promptly every morning
in the schedule of their lives;
they rarely fare beyond
the garden gate, gliding down
the washing-line on a hand-looped
cleaning rag, like dangling
from a strap-rail in a tram.
Leaded windows are then
vented, wiped, the grime
removed from painted sills.

Overnight intrusions
(cat depositing a half-chewed bird,
litter cast by careless passer-by)
are quickly tidied out of sight
before they tour the inside
of their lives, take down
and dust from moth-proof shelves
framed family photographs,
vases, brassware, figurines;
to overtake the pressing
haste of time, determined
not to leave themselves behind.

AUNT GLADYS
(victim of the influenza
epidemic of 1919, aged 22)

Her life as it might have been
lies here in this unwritten book
releasing virgin pages
to the messengers of time;
recording only sketches for
a life from chance remarks
of those who knew her well
and cherished in her echoed prime.

'How graceful, how like a flower
she hung upon her father's arm.'

This, and sundry details
culled from lives sprung up
and thrived around her, tell
of where she lived, and how,
and in what time her beauty
yielded to the rare-ripe scythe.

AUNT MAGGIE

The public wash-house
flourished on the meaner side
of town, its doors flung open
like the jaws of some inferno
belching heat and steam.

Laundry loaded on a pram,
she pushed it Friday nights
through shrinking streets,
against the paler human tide
winding home from cotton mills.

Husband Harry, in his prime,
sauntered slowly up the hill
sweating out the foundry grime,
his oil-stained flannel shirt
unbuttoned to a red kerchief.

Obsessive it was with her
to get his charcoal linen clean
of dirt seared daily into it;
and return, before the advent
of the full front-load machine.

BEHIND THE SHOP

A bottle of strong stout
regaled the supper table,
its haul of fish and chips
they sent me out to fetch.

Grandma, firmly matriarchal,
sat with hair brushed back
in the tight, fastidious bun
adorning all her widowhood.

In the stuffed aquarium
exhibition perch and chub
drifted round the watery walls
towards the setting sun.

On the rambling garden walk,
deep mysterious holding tanks
stood dark and lean and dank,
their denizens long gone.

It stretched back endlessly
in my child-enchanted eye;
its green forbidden reaches,
the all-conspiring sky.

And the shop itself selling
live bait, rods and flies,
recalled its owner's style
in gold medals and charred pipes.

DISUSED BRANCH LINE

These tracks lead from us
to some unknown destination,
escaping their own future
among the loosestrife, willow herb,
the worn and sunken sleepers:
a standing invitation
we have not kept to journeys
we might once have made
in lame intent to visit
absent friends, new towns,
distant near relations.

Departing from the pressing plan
—*horaire des trains*—
that grips us to set rails
we dare not leave for fear
the running of our lives
will shunt back on ourselves;
switching us from safer,
sure connections, fixed routines,
our scheduled discontents.
These tracks lead on to empty fires
on long-abandoned stations.

COUNCIL FLATS

They stand in tower blocks
against the sullen backdrop
of the late-November sky,
vying for a corner in the sun.

A thin partition screens them
from the limply-hanging air:
a threadbare coat a beggar wears
in hostage to the elements.

The lower part is made of wood
daubed with rough graffiti;
the paler surface of the glass
reflects a hungering for love.

Dividing walls are thin enough
to hear the winning argument,
absorb the impact of adjacent lives
lived this side of paradise.

Some reserve of grass between
each plot, some planted trees,
their souls might swiftly blossom,
the startled birds might sing.

THE FACE OF CHANGE
(*Oldham, Lancashire*)

On this commercial plain,
one may still watch the plow
slow-laboring up the hill,
as in any rural county;
from the lane I see it now.

Not far behind the plow,
a dense flock of gulls
descends from a clearing sky
on new-turned strips of earth,
to pick among the stones.

On an arc of green hill
where grass is close-cropped,
a chestnut lithely strides;
hooves reduce the ground,
fetlocks brush the sky.

This mill town, a birdcall
from the tilled field's rim,
face tight-set to a future,
yet clings to the vestiges
of a past industrialism.

THE RIVER IRK
(*Chadderton, Lancs*)

This simple watercourse
has long been here
soaking its bracken soul
before the Celts set foot
on the higher ground
surmounting all the marsh around.

Not much to shout about
on its few miles of lonely life
from foothills of the Pennines
to the Irwell's silent mouth;
except a small secluded park
laid out with formal lawns,
paved walks and flower beds,
where the medieval hall
stood mellowing its honeyed walls.

Now a natural aspect
is re-created on its banks,
with a thin stand of birches,
the wildnesses of grass;
here, too, the peaceful water
only once in modern times
reached high above itself
and snatched a man.

Death's hint of drama too is lost
when the river quits this wild, idyllic spot
to join the toilers in the town,
where they discount its rural past
with quaint, discarded artifacts:
worn tyres, split mattresses and prams
they fished the baby out of long ago.

INNER-CITY CHURCH
(*Manchester*)

Its stone walls reflect
the pale autumnal light;
its tall Gothic spire
punctuates the sky
like an exclamation mark.

A solitary priest
wanders the aisles inside
on a blind lead plugged
in somewhere, bearing
flowers for loved ones.

Outside, the passers-by
have different rituals,
daily set routines leaving
little time to spare for
elusive supernaturals.

Women trip to pews
alone, un-chaperoned,
on some blind date
they wait for patiently,
met by scent and music.

BLACKPOOL IN WINTER

Morning sun bursts through,
to bathe the vast champaigns
of sand in oceanic light.

Pied oyster-catchers throng
to the wide receding tide,
the lip of the feeding sea.

In lifting fog the pier-end
looms like the fo'c's'le of a ship
surreptitiously entering dock.

Inland, pale intimations
of the famous pleasure beach
weave around skeletal steel

of roller-coasters begun in
the mind, but swiftly aborted,
misted, cliff-edged, blind.

Beyond South Pier the town,
sea front, tower and promenade
slip into winter's hinterland.

Guest houses, arcades, bars
hold their gusto in reserve,
pigeonholed, adjourned.

THE PREACHER
(St. Margaret's, Hollinwood)

He ascends the pulpit steps,
half-suspended between earth
and those celestial regions
he half-credibly describes.

His congregation stay below,
in the pit of their own lives,
exhorted by his chosen words
to raise themselves half up
in hope for one brief moment
of something greater, more
enduring than themselves.

Stone of wall and pillar echo
hollowly his theme, stressing
in their stubborn materiality
the illusion of earthly things
his task is to inspire beyond,
leaving them with restive feet
anticipating treading clouds.

They go home to Sunday roasts
and the week-long material grind,
setting their feet firmly back
in the humdrum of their lives;
in the long, labored walk
between the earth that draws them
and the overwhelming sky.

ROOD SCREEN
(St. James's, Oldham)

I saw this tree standing
bare on thieves' Calvary,
outside the living walls,
in the known place of skulls.

It held the stench of death
around it, raging round
the numbing nostrils of those
with abject hanging faces;

veiled and weeping women,
sullen guards who louder grew
dividing the spoils of one more.
And now the curious few

who turned up for a miracle
slunk dispiritedly away,
down to the foot of the hill
and the city's lustier smells.

It was a kind of non-event
for them, a usual execution
with a subtle difference one
could not put a finger on.

Yet that bare tree grew vines:
that was not blood, but wine;
and that wine was not wine,
but letting, living blood.

BLACKPOOL PIER

It strides out to sea
on unlimited legs
that will not give out
when incoming waves
assail the long shore.

It lends the illusion
of extending the land
enclosed by high walls
withholding the strand
from the sea's elopement.

Strolling the pier
is a mystical journey,
its length determined
by surfaced ambitions
to walk on water.

It goes one step further
on the midsummer circuit
that hurries us here:
to commune with the sea
at a tactical distance.

ABINGDON

The old Benedictine spirit
subtly pervades this place
picturesquely complementing
upper reaches of the Thames.

Evoked by watching owls,
it loiters in extensive grounds
surrounding the abbey ruins
and the modern market town.

It clings to the stone walls
of the brothers' water-mill;
the wheel still slowly turns,
no longer grinding corn.

At evening settled streets
feeding the deserted square
regain the lingering peace
of cloister, compline, cowl.

Across the river meadows,
by oak, sycamore and beech,
almshouses and an inn
mark the parish of St. Helen.

MONASTERY LIBRARY

It has long been compiling,
volume by antique volume,
this learning of centuries;
its free-range speculation
we reserve for ourselves.

Behind the high shelves,
quieter than cloisters,
we have acquired the habit
of hoarding this treasure,
its incorruptible pearls.

Sermons of John Donne,
a medieval Book of Hours,
lie innocently cheek by jowl
with the fleshier heresies
we surreptitiously browse.

We have not lost the habit
at Vespers of taking them
down; our writings from here,
distilled in the stillness,
break new Divine ground.

BROTHER ANSELM

He was advanced in age,
well past three score and ten,
patient, accepting and serene
in the fullness of his years.

Becoming old,
he grew slowly more alone;
here, in the community of Brothers
active in their teaching lives,
he felt a growing isolation
stalking the halls of the school
he had chalked for forty years.

At the end there was little
beyond the knowing loneliness
of his celibate profession;
denied family ties, his kin
were more or less this same
community of men, each
in his active, dedicated life.

I felt this as he turned on me
his gently inward smile,
pressed me to a second mug
of coffee at the bell to start
the term-time afternoon.
His brothers briefly left him
to his growing share of less;
yet I sensed no bitterness.

STEEPLES

They rise up from the pagan earth,
from any landscape, taking shape
according to an age or local style.

They scrape the base of clouds,
lofting our mundane aspirations
to some high celestial ground.

Each village has its particular spire,
its own petition for a better harvest,
victory, or some other social good.

Each country has an individual
tongue; a close identity with God,
who never failed to take their side

in just or unjust wars against
good Christian adversaries;
united under threat of minaret.

Viewed from above they might be
pin-pricks, or even spines on
some porcupine bristling at God.

Or solemn signposts out of time,
erecting in cement and stone
sharp pointers to the undefined.

EVENING AT DARTMOUTH
(*Devon*)

The ferry passes inexorably
between two fixed points,
discharging cargoes
to unfixed journeys picked
with headlamps in the night.

This full-rigged yacht moored
at the river wall has scaled
the swell of mounting seas;
looks old in timber beside
the chrome and fibre-glass

of motley weekend craft
chained to this threshold
of the sea, in the dark pool
beyond shallow harbor lights,
the taverns tilting on sea-legs.

The tide unfurls between
twin keeps struggling to pen
the unknown within known bounds;
to stay the life-stream drifting out
to the drowning sea.

DEVON SHORE

Here in the bay of all desire
the sea drifts out to meet the sky,
far from the cry of inland cities,
the crowding lives; here
at the birth of all our days
the combing waves slide back
the golden age of sand.

The shore climbs back
by adder track, to reach
the listing cliff-top farm;
its crumbling walls owe little
to our metric laws, our set desire
to get the angles right before
we build the fastness of our souls.

Behind the farm and through
the fields the hawthorn lane
disperses hamlets on its way,
ambles on and loops at will.
It matters not, for time is slow;
and slower still, the grazing herd
reshapes the brinded contours of the hill.

ISLE OF WIGHT

Here is an emerald island
in the bay, sunlight reflecting
in the hollows of the waves,
enveloping in sheets of
spilling sail that run
the open gauntlet to the sea.

What does the island say,
when islands speak a tongue
consistently beyond
the eavesdrop of the land?

It reveals some surface
secrets on the way: birds
that nest in jagged clefts;
wild flowers that grow
in tangled hedgerows;
headland trails rising
in the teeth of biting gales;
chalk cliffs descending
to the salt sea-lanes.

HOLIDAYMAKERS
(Isle of Wight)

They gaze across the empty
places of the sea, eager faces
awaiting sundry occupation;
like sea-view boarding houses
with rooms like vacant eyes.

Their recent past has suddenly
deserted them, transcribed them
to this other time; émigrés
for a short season running
all the length of promenades.

They pale before the task of
quickly building second lives,
finding routine things to do,
discovering favorite haunts
amid transcendent novelty.

Slowly the local tan arrives
to re-export, to naturalize;
days it takes them fully
to acclimatize to all this
new potential, this surprise.

GIRL SUNBATHING

Stretched out on the beach,
she may attract or repel;
my mildly disconcerted gaze
takes umbrage in the sand.

She turns, half-done;
firm, sun-bronzed hills
and cryptic vales are focused
in a well-splayed land.

Our eyes fleetingly meet:
only by her due consent
do I now have leave to linger
past convention's bounds.

This firm, vital flesh,
projecting a rude health,
masks its toll of sickness
and attendant veils of age.

I love it as I love myself,
in its literal statement
of revealing truth: witness,
candidness and youth.

NEXUS

Each place creates
its own sense of exile,
if we have been there
only once, or known it
nearly all our lives.

It holds back something
of itself, of mystery,
of ethos; that elusive
spirit of community
we dare to share.

As we reserve
part of ourselves,
never fully committed;
plotting to escape
on weekend breaks.

Our home town
merely deceives us least,
with the sham familiarity
of known streets;
with the addictive smile.

LEAVING HARWICH BY TRAIN

Cars are racing to the coast,
to Harwich and the onward boats;
escaping down the Suffolk lanes,
the scenery is much the same.

Horsepower harnessed to its wheels,
the boat-train ploughs,
through fleeting stubble fields,
a furrow straighter than an arrow.

It rides above the supple hedge
and tunnels deep into the womb
of country that may not remain
long in this rich and settled vein.

Low the fenland marshes lie,
ribbed with ditch and sea canal;
a copse surmounts the broken hill
skirting the wide city's overspill.

Cars are racing to the coast,
to Harwich and returning boats;
only the Channel stems the flow
of fields as green as England.

OFF PADSTOW
(*Cornwall*)

Sails assemble on the tide,
straggling the wide estuary
from Stepper Point to Pentire.

Intrepid, they leave the quay
in speedboats heading out
to Puffin Island in the sea.

Staid vacationers prefer
the ferry's gentler wetting,
salt breeze waving hair.

Down the blowing coastal mile,
fishing vessels skim the bay's
harvest of forgotten smiles.

A dredger tugs at anchor-chain;
a letter-day *Marie-Celeste*,
its crew has slipped away.

The ebb tide sets us on the crest
of depths receding waves addressed.

LLANDUDNO
(*North Wales*)

Seagulls pierce the morning air
with raucous cries across
the roofs of waterfront hotels.

The tide folds in its even length
across the shingle sloping shore,
obliterating yesterday, and sandy lore.

Cloudships fill the ocean sky,
scudding forth—the sea drifts by—
oblivious of sail below.

People stare from windows pale,
gauging weather, sighting whale,
before they start the chill parade
along the windswept promenade.

BOWLERS AT LLANELLI
(South Wales)

Eight woods against the jack,
ten jacks across the green;
forty players of uneven age,
clad in deference to the game
(white slacks, cotton shirts,
dapper wide-neb bowling caps),
solemnly address the nap.

Rituals are well observed
by these Sabbath artisans
honing the highlights of the game;
coaxing the biased bowl along
with quasi-prayerful motions,
urging its curved trajectory
to within a clinching inch.

On hushed tip-toe they run up
behind each balanced throw;
shouting in loud hyperbole
some ultimate instruction;
cherishing their rivals' play;
loving their own company
in the hallowed all-male way.

BATSMAN ON TOUR

When he stepped up to the crease
he became, not so much himself,
but a carver of dreams for viewers
well beyond the boundary fence;

the embodiment of collective will
to meet the challenge deep within
ourselves, redress deep-seated
failures in the national psyche,

restore us to respect and pride
on foreign fields before the sun-
baked hostile crowds, fallibility
of umpires, fickleness of bounce.

Success won him the laurel crown,
failure saw it wither on his brow;
only our dreams are not deceived;
they merely ride the next bat out.

DRAMATIC SEAM BOWLER
(England v. Australia 1993 Test Series)

He strolls into the wings,
rehearsing sotto voce;
turns and gathers pace,
the restless crowd behind him
like a harrying wind.

Each voiceless delivery
is its own piece of theatre,
articulately pitched to draw
the Hamlet batsman
out onto center stage;

get him to commit himself
to a reading of the script,
when each fresh delivery
varies almost imperceptibly
in nuance, speed and drift.

A sharp, tense blade
flashes in bright sunlight;
an edge to second slip,
a broad, declaiming hit:
the drama is the play.

SWITZERLAND

It lives as much in the mind
as in the everyday world.

Refugees fondly pictured it,
fleeing Nazi Germany;

as did French Huguenots
after St. Batholomew's Eve.

Einstein here conceived
a revolution in physics.

Lenin plotted another,
less scientific, coup

from his Zurich apartment
with a St. Petersburg view.

Carl Gustav Jung plumbed
the depths of the mind,

the human personality,
universal archetypes.

Scaling its high peaks
is an alpinist's dream;

the Museum of Chocolate
gets most of the cream.

ZURICH

Narrow streets wind upwards
from the waterfront arcades,
raising vermeil rooftops to
the gardens of the Lindenhof.

Peeling bells ring out across
the city's medieval heart,
a gull's lacustrine dart
along the Bahnhofstrasse,

Europe's most expensive street,
bank and boutique broking gold,
fine art and furs; café-crème
with *kuchen* and conserves.

From spreading lake the Limmat
rushes to escape the channels
of its history: floodlit guidlhalls,
the Reformation Water Church.

It skips nocturnal Niederdorf,
its bouquet of bratwurst,
Turkish coffee, roasted snails;
the ambivalence of love for sale.

COMPOSITION OF A EUROPEAN CITY

Sober, tonic Zurich
is the compelling music
of Johann Sebastian Bach.

Flights of stone steps
form interrupted cadences
behind baroque facades.

Counterpoint of spires
soar silently above cantatas
sung by four-part choirs.

Roof gardens in the *Altstadt*
are delicate embellishments,
floral grace notes.

Neat, sequestered squares
hear music students playing
partitas for solo violin.

Rodin's *Gate of Hell*
augments a scene from the Creed,
the *Symbolum Nicenum*.

Trams are blue *glissandi*
gliding down repeated streets
to upland pastorales.

TOUR OF JAMES JOYCE

A vintage tram hauls steeply
from the lake, glides past
the Schauspielhaus: think of
English theatre, English plays
diplomatically staged.

He might have caught it
many times commuting
from the Limmatquai
to the seedy tenements
with a genteel view
through faded lace;
a plaque set in the wall:
Here lived James Joyce . . .
next door is a pizza place.

The tram swings high
to scale the valley side;
on open heath where
Bengal tigers roam
(inside the zoo),
the people's army
trains its youth to make
the imaginary kill and break
the spell of Sunday afternoon.

The terminus a sunlit glade;
in a tranquil corner under trees
he himself might choose to read,
a small bronze figure spreads
an open book: could be *Ulysses.*
Here lies James Joyce . . .
among the lettered graves.

STEPPENWOLF
(Hermann Hesse, 1926)

He left cold rooms
on the Schanzengraben
to attend masked balls
at Hotel Baur au Lac;
his forced merriment
was itself a charade,
to veil ingrained despair.

The seductive embrace
of girls dissembling love
in the riot of Carnival nights,
escaping into the dawn,
was the cruelest charade;
at these rites of youth,
he felt betrayed by age.

In Zurich of the twenties,
he was a creature living
on the fringes of society,
a loner, an outsider
who belied his status
as sage, romantic writer;
working his life into his art.

VIOLON D'AUTOMNE

Six o'clock:
the keys of the clavecin
in the window of the shop
selling antique instruments
emphatically stopped.

Our evening meal
began with tepid soup
at your modest *pension*
a fox-trot farther on,
just past the Limmatplatz.

It was the only time
you invited me to share
such intimate occasion,
between the semi-breves;
the chestnut trees were bare.

How deceived I was
by this staged departure
from your cool reserve;
how ensnared by strawberry hair
fluting through the square.

MUNSTERHOF
(*Zurich*)

Can more be said in stone
than this Baroque city square
harmoniously declares
in muted pastel tones?

Pure eloquence flows,
from medieval guildhall
to Fraumunster's secure walls
that sheltered Huguenots.

St. Peter's painted clock
arrests tourists' attention:
as time goes, time stands still,
locked in a bygone century.

The River Limmat holds
its rapid, lake-fed course
beneath low bridges strolled
by gulls and city-goers.

Beyond its runic shores,
stone builds again heroically
on stone, in the twin-spired
Romanesque Grossmunster.

VISITING THE CATHEDRAL
J'ai visité la cathédrale
Auguste Rodin

We are visiting the cathedral
of Limburg, newly repainted
the color of flesh, a dark
sunburned flesh that contrasts
starkly with the skeleton inside.

Here is its authentic age:
along the quiet nave footfall
and voice are long hushed,
the bare bones are blanched,
the texture is of sudden dust.

In this colonnade of limbs,
femurs and the girded thighs
stride the huge ribbed edifice
aloft amid this world of wars
and through the bloodshot sky.

This was not the cathedral
visited by Rodin in respites
from sittings in stone or bronze;
his cathedral was of living flesh:
it was his mistress, idealized.

WETZLAR

An urgent figure in a dark
frock-coat mysteriously appears
against the old stone bridge
across wide reaches of the Lahn,
a legal tome beneath his arm.

The city has ancestral calm
beneath the windows leaning
over mottled streets, buildings
lovingly restored in bright
half-timbers where gables meet.

The gaunt cathedral to his left
in *son et lumiere*, he climbs
against the awkward camber
of the cobbled square; pauses
at the fountain for a drink.

He knocks at the narrow door
that gives onto a leafy court
sequestering the burgher's home,
its stone-floored kitchen where
he sat to eat beneath the stairs.

In the time-repining boudoir
Lotte's presence is preserved
in letters, clothes and cameos,
the perfumed dressing-table,
the ornate way she did her hair.

The salon furniture sits still;
no ghost has turned a hair
since Goethe's youthful visits
there two hundred years ago,
a law student with a lover's brief.

A GRANDMOTHER'S BIRTHDAY
(*Wetzlar*)

She greets us smiling
across the tiled floor of her parlor
huddling many guests between
the window and the burning stove.

Generations take their turn
before the mounds of *kuchen,*
torten and the bristling hams,
a glass of schnapps to hand.

The wage-earners eat first,
laconic men with large appetites
who know the high seriousness
of eating as they understand

the value of their daily toil.
They cede to the stiff elders,
dignified in suit and tie; one
remembered England from the war.

Another dearly lost his wife,
spent his time whittling wood,
filling the void and his home
with carved substitutes for love.

When these had slowly eaten
and withdrawn, the patient women
quit the kitchen and their aprons,
poured fresh coffee and sat down.

Grossmutter partook of little;
she sat smiling serenely
in the blessings of her years,
fussed the children and felt proud.

DUSSELDORF

Something drew me
to the tranquil riverside,
thinking of Robert Schumann;
in the grip of his delirium,
he here attempted suicide.

A brain tumor causing
musical hallucinations,
he requested sequestration
in a Bonn asylum, to protect
Clara Wieck, his wife.

A stranger here might feel,
as in any large new city,
a kindred isolation,
stranded like a traffic island
in the circulating lives.

The wilder, navigable river
had a defined sense
of purpose, of direction;
amid a man-made ambience,
it had an elemental mind.

A telling lust for life,
as in soulful song
or fresh-pressed wine,
spills out in this composer's
Third Symphony: *The Rhine*.

THE SUNKEN JETTY
(*Starnbergersee, Bavaria*)

A young woman
in a long white skirt
with matching blouse,
a parasol,
steps into the waiting boat;
her escort reaches out
a gallant hand,
to steady her.

She sits astern,
dreamily twirling
the unfurled parasol,
head tilted slightly back;
she smiles serenely
at the perfection of scenery,
the idyll of the day across
the summer surface of the lake.

Drifting,
her hand trails lightly
through the water,
causing just the faintest
rippled wake.
She looks into the eyes
of her beloved,
a sadly gentle
but expectant smile
before the ripples fade.

The water settles smoothly
over them, covering the jetty.

ZELL AM SEE

The lake lies quite shallow
at its pebbled northern edge,
like an ornamental pond
with mallards and a lone swan.

Yet it could draw down
high peaks into its depths:
the Kitzsteinhorn yawning,
the Pinzgau sharply etched.

Its still waters have a stint
of dense, organic green,
reflecting sturdy spruce and fir
crowding this alpine scene.

On summer afternoons,
bathers seek a sloping beach
at the coldly-lapping edge
of a glacial feeder stream.

A stand of silver birches
screens upscale, reclusive villas
peeping out between the trees
at lake, alp, recurring dream.

OSTEND
(*Belgium*)

From Ostend, gateway to
the eastern Rhine, their sudden
haste searches sun-south;

escapes the clinging breezes
of this harbor town, an island
once by the channeled sea

basking the sandy beaches
to the shallow reaches
of the Andromeda Hotel.

Drinks across drifting tables
sip through helix of cigars:
they come here yearly

not to leave but to imbibe
the pleasures of the Lido
flushed, fleshed-out between
the waffles and the sun-washed sea.

AT THE SEA WALL
(*Ostend*)

Whitecaps start far out;
they come racing in as if the sea,
uncontained by its huge metre,
were escaping from itself.

It leaves us little beyond
the dampening patch that marks
a pattern of insistent reach,
and a thin black line of mussels

for the mottled gulls that stand
a calculated distance from its path;
it will snatch back anything
we leave within its grasp.

Life, they say, first surfaced
in the sea: we roam like exiles
in a banished land; return,
compulsive, to the sea's drawn edge

to glean its sealed horizons
in our mesh of discontent.
Raging spent, the sea recoils
replete, entire, abated, spent.

LOBSTERS AT OSTEND

They still imagine a life,
escaping across the blue-sea
surreal floor of the holding tank
outside the seafood restaurant
a short hop from the beach.

Morning sun casts shadows
on their fancied flight,
in their small gratis aquarium
fed by the constant oxygen's
clear, deceiving stream.

Antennae sounding suspect depths,
they yet engage bound claws
in skirmish over margins
none can win, but all must cede
to new arrivals off the evening boat.

By then they will encompass
strange, eclectic china seas,
uncharted reefs awash with Muscadet
that lie quite unsuspected, unimagined
round a corner of their compound eye.

NIGHT FERRY FROM STOCKHOLM

We sail into the calmest sea,
of waves that roll like icing
on a wedding cake, prow carving
this nocturnal feast, lit not

by festive bridal lights, but in
the watery echoes of the moon
extending all this eerie night
to the brink of fast horizons,

to wooded, ice-locked islands
in the Finnish archipelago.
We stroll the deck ignoring cold,
the thin night breeze off this

suspended sea we might with ease
slip down to, skate or ski above
the waves through frozen fields
of deep midwinter snowdrops.

HELSINKI

Granite outcrops punctuate
the spartan statement of this
Baltic city entered by the sea.

Ash-blond girls emerge
gift-wrapped in furs from
reindeer restaurants snowbound

near the quay where sailing boats
re-berth in spring and sea-blown
farmers sell their hard-won produce

from island craft slipped in among
ocean-going liners bound for
Stockholm, Riga and Tallinn.

Two cathedrals, Orthodox
and Lutheran, stand mute
before the witness of the bay,

reflecting in rival piety
the divided loyalty of the Finn,
between the West and the emerging East.

RIITTA

She had dark eyes
and this Latin name that seemed
incongruous in the teeth of winter
blanketing snow.

Oriental fabrics
clothed bare walls with magic,
in her small room by the harbor's
easterly flow.

A handloom crowded the corner,
thread hung limply in abeyance
to uncompleted studies
at the Athenaeum.

Half-answered letters
strewed the table,
easing the night of days,
her Nordic sense of isolation.

Russian filters mixed with incense
burning for some eastern atman
close to her migrating soul,
far from Finland.

SAUNA ON THE ROOF OF THE PALACE HOTEL

Sweat-wet skin
clings like an ice-coat,
close-fitting.

Up-rush of blue
from the white harbor
singes nerve-ends
at open pores: sensuous,
this chilling nudity suspends
above the fur-clad walkways
of the city.

Down-gaze escalates
through twelve floors
of thinning space,
above the milling insects
on a Baltic carapace.

Dry heat
draws us nimbly back
through penthouse doors,
to thaw out brittle limbs
in pinewood kilns.

THE FINNISH NORTH

Sense the purity of this land,
its taut brown earth blending
north to the Barents Sea,

drifting through dry embers
of leaves flickering red and gold
on the autumn-turning tundra.

Penetrate the tense virginity
of trees clearing to birched skin
by the lakeside torpid sauna.

Roll over in packed snow,
while lean sausages are grilling
on smooth stove-top stones.

Admire the wrested humor
of its forest folk fashioning
logs with frozen hands.

ICE-FISHING ON LAKE OULU

One frozen smock clung
dry land to the lake,
beyond human cry, wisp
of smoke from pine dwelling.

We set out on our skis
along deep forest trails;
skimmed the packed ice
to a point beyond distance.

Pitched camp with hot coffee
and bent to the spade's
unremitting descent
to winter-locked waves.

Sank line with small bait
into the lake's dark belly,
probing its depths
from the brink of our day;

resurrecting the life
locked under the ice,
now drawn to its death
in the banqueting sun.

VIRPI

Tall she stood among pines,
lean as the white birch
that grew along outcrops
on the side of the gorge

where the river deepened
before the high dam,
its obtrusive mass
soon drowned in the taiga.

Fair she stood and waiting,
on shifting ground between
school and employment
in wintry cities of the south:

grey knots of buildings
hemmed in by lakes,
foreign to her woodland soul,
its homage to the wild.

Waiting for some passing stranger
to resolve her keen dilemma;
offering meanwhile the blaze
of her hearth, birch-bark of her skin.

VIEW OF STOCKHOLM

It stands over a mirror
gazing down into its past:
a statuesque Narcissus
in self-absorbing mask.

Mirror spreads and deepens,
framed by the granite rock;
veering the weekend sailors
into the skerried loch.

Ships slide in their masts
beside the tall Riksdag;
they set the Baltic voyager
on instant winding paths.

Winter dims the mirror
to a silver, frosted mass;
children skating over
etch paradigms on glass.

The sun hastens to sunset
beyond the Skagerak;
day deserts its verges,
night comes crowding back.

VISIT TO LENINGRAD

His most cogent memory
was a bunch of wildflowers
a young woman gave him,
coming fresh that day
from a windswept trip
to the birch country.

Surprised him with them,
taking final leave
of a group of students
on the Nevsky Prospekt,
where it sauntered past
the Park of Culture and of Rest.

Past stores that caught
the late consumer tide
rising through the dusk;
and lengthening queues
at sidewalk symphony
and theatre ticket booths.

By crowds that overflowed
the teeming streets,
veering north towards
the rolling River Neva,
its long-receding vistas
of a tsarist Russia.

ALEKSANDR BORODIN

Composition was for him
a kind of *violon d'Ingres*
to his scientific work
at St. Petersburg University;
he would be on sick-leave,
often streaming with a cold,
as he approached the keyboard.

His ready attentiveness
to the needs of others,
especially young students
who bent his willing ear
with their various concerns,
took a further toll of his
time and resources.

By nature modest,
he questioned his ability,
when shown the scenario
of the epic *Prince Igor*,
devoting two decades
to this operatic masterpiece
without completing the score.

In the celebrated
nineteenth-century tradition
of the brilliant amateur,
he brought to his task
no hint of dilletantism,
but the highest of motives,
that of *amator* or lover.

CRUISING THE DANUBE
(in the wake of the Cold War)

It augurs ill to watch them
take with rods the measured
depth of water in the river's
upper reaches after drought.

Buda slices neat in half
from Pest; and where the Belvaros
runs furtive alleys to the high,
Turk-repulsing battlements,

the boat peacefully docks.
It sails upon an early tide
through the sharp defile
of high Carpathians lurking

sturgeon in ink-black pools.
Languidity of days extends
to scented nights in garden
restaurants where the river stops.

Beyond Belgrade advance
the flood-plains of Romania;
in stricken towns they salvage
what the water-level left.

The Danube now has lost
its other bank; we are hailed
afar by southern flags that fly
this ocean river to the sea.

WORSHIPPERS AT BUCHAREST, 1970

They stand before the icon
in the narthex of a monastery
church, stooping women with
gnarled hands, black shawls.

In creaking file they crawl
with ancient patience taking
each her turn to touch or kiss
the gilded image on the wall.

It holds this focal power in
their lives the state derides;
speaks to them in the intimate
insistencies of candle-glow;

in undertones of shadows
flickering on the tallow stone.
Eyes are still and passive,
stylized in the old iconic art

of revealing almost nothing;
an eternal self-assurance
asking little of believers,
yet at length demanding all.

SIMONE WEIL
(1909-1943)

A lesson of her short life
might be this: to spurn
convention; not to seek
refuge in it, as many do,
sometimes unconsciously,
building lean lives upon it,
calculating each step
of a conventional career.

But to act emphatically
on each new impulse
that might suddenly arise,
even if wildly impractical:
her scheme to airlift nurses
into the troops' front line;
the strikes she organized
among the unemployed.

Living among the poor,
she spurned private means
to identify with them;
stripped of her dignity,
she regained it painfully,
discovering a humanity
stripped of externals,
the barest human worth.

She remained outside
any recognized church,
raising private conscience
above tribal conformity;
to die unbaptised,
while believing in Christ,
on the same cross of war
that crucified France.

DIETRICH BONHOEFFER:
Letters & Papers from Prison (1943-45)

Composed on paper scraps
slipped past the warders,
they record a ministry
to his fellow prisoners
closely packed in airless
upper rooms at Buchenwald,
the nights of Allied raids.

They reveal his humanity
and a warmth of friendship
not now to be renewed,
despite unflinching faith
in the justice of his case;
his conviction of a sure
release arriving any day.

They display an appetite
for books, feeding his mind
on Goethe, Plutarch, Barth
towards the day of liberation,
the world beyond the war;
outlined in scholarly debate
his modern, skeptic faith.

And portray a lucid thinker
on the issues of the day,
a youthful zest for life,
love of art and music,
of the roving countryside;
enjoyment of a good cigar,
but do not mention wine.

NICE
(*French Riviera*)

Sawn heads of martyrs
frame the cloistered garden
where we spend Franciscan evenings
at summer concerts in the scented air.

From tonsured hill the town unfolds
in pastel tones the contours of its soul;
we pause for *pastis* or *citron*
at tables by the English Promenade.

Bodies turning in the sun
ripen for the evening trade
in olive skin and vin rosé,
beneath the palm trees' horizontal sway.

Crabs are caught in bouillabaisse
dredging up through antique waters,
where the still-life quayside restaurants
front the wide Ligurian Bay.

VILLAGERS ON THE LOIRE

Despite the dry fact
that it often threatens
to overwhelm them,
they do not want
the river dammed,
its courses changed.

In Auvergne,
they see nature untamed:
a red kite slowly hoisting,
a kingfisher stringing
close to the current's thread,
above the watershed.

For them beauty,
the high, wild beauty
of the Upper Loire
deepening through gorges,
coursing by vineyards,
is on a par with life itself.

The river is life
to a whole environment,
on which everything
in harmony depends;
acknowledging this,
it's the beauty they defend.

VENICE

Watching in the dim glow
of San Marco, before the icons,
we feel the tread of time
in sinking flagstones at our feet.

Mandatory gondola ride
glides us down the lapping lanes
to the highway Grand Canal
marshalling these silent cars

beneath high arch or balcony
overhanging water-street;
returning by the Bridge of Sighs
condemning men to chains.

The most bracing trip by far,
to see Murano glass, heads past
San Michele, island of the dead,
in backwash of the water-hearse,

which leaves its silent cargo
at the waiting steps, beyond
the call of loved ones left
bereft across the broad lagoon.

MOUNT ETNA

Earth regurgitates,
heaving seething innards
up through jaws of fire
gaping high above
the Mediterranean Sea,
scene of many cataclysms.

The Atlantic poured in
its threefold Niagara
through the Pillars of Hercules
millions of years ago,
where continents met
at the Straits of Gibraltar.

The sea became
a haven for sperm whales,
a playground for dolphins;
for those who, wide-eyed,
roam its olive shores
on packaged summer holidays,

little dreaming
on the sun-baked surface
of the hour of such anarchic
events linking us through time
to the spiral ammonite
whorled by the turning tide.

ALEXANDRIA OLD TOWN

Neat are the cobbled streets
laid down by working gangs
of Hessian soldiers captured
in the War of Independence.

They lead you steeply
past flowering cherry-trees
to the vast, expansive flow
of the old Potomac River

sporting a small marina
for weekend motor-yachts
and a deeper outside berth
for a vintage paddle-steamer.

One engaging structure,
of crushed oyster shells,
fittingly now serves as
thriving quayside diner:

octopus, swordfish, shark,
stewed alligator parts,
form a deep-trawled foil
to routine gourmet arts.

Picture galleries abound
in views of schooner ports
from old colonial times
on inlets like Jamestown.

OGUNQUIT
(*Maine*)

When the east wind
suddenly stiffened
kites became brigantines
under colorful sail,
dipping fitfully
like rudderless ships
in the troughs of waves;
or bobbing aloft
on billows of cloud.

A hound at their heels,
a young boy and a girl
raced over the sands
of the oystered bay,
kite-string playing
like a running anchor chain,
wind swimming their hair,
free from parental care,
adrift for the day.

Staid elders sat
content in deckchairs,
or took brisk walks
by nesting dunes;
breakers crashed
upon the open strand
besieged by seagulls
pecking shellfish,
as by darting sanderlings.

SANDERLINGS

While his fellows scurry
to and fro at the tide's edge,
pecking at shellfish,
the sanderling with one leg
competes with the best of them;
legless he'd be dead.

Which is why, presumably,
we are given two
of many working parts,
to remain operational
facing mishap or disease;
a fail-safe, if you please.

Uniqueness, in a sense,
demands unique defense:
a helmet for the skull,
cod-piece, rib-cage
(to protect the heart);
headless, we'd be dead.

WINDSURFER ON LAKE WINNISQUAM
(*New Hampshire*)

He picked his time,
in pale evening light,
as the stiff wind roiled
the coiled expanse.

The hungry lake,
licking solid rock,
nibbling gulls' wings,
winnowing dense weeds,

soon swallowed him,
in a trick of distance
from the peeling shore.
His slender craft

pitched starboard,
its tall, falling sail
displacing him.
Floundering,

like a porpoise netted,
he scrambled free,
clambered back aboard,
his wet-suit wetted;

began again to test
his mettle, his resolve
to read the fickle mind
of wind and wave.

THE GRAND HOTELS
(*White Mountains, NH*)

Conceived in the age
of steam railways,
they catered to the needs
of the rich and famous
trading intense city heat
for a mountain retreat.

It was an age, too,
of the belated discovery
of the joys of scenery;
Victoria built Balmoral
in the Scottish highlands;
the Swiss equipped the alps.

Few establishments
advertised in the press,
relying on recommendation
from well-heeled patrons
to draw society clients
for the summer season.

Their heyday is long gone,
following two world wars,
social upheavals,
the ubiquitous automobile,
the ethos of the beach,
package tours abroad.

ARIZONANS

They spread well out
along wide boulevards
with neat, greening verges
on the tailored outskirts of the town.

Next door the desert blooms
in multitudes of undiscovered secrets
that resist due integration
into an air-conditioned world.

Beyond the potted cacti
and the ornamental palms,
sky looms azure over mesas
and the mesquite steppe.

In all this amplifying silence,
the deafened desert lurks;
it will strike back with scorpions
when the sprinklers stop.

THE ARTS

Art begins where Nature ends
                    Marc Chagall (1887-1985)

RUSSIAN FIGURE SKATER

Flowing through
athletic set routines,
'the required elements',
Olga is cool as ice.

The pursuing music
is of Scriabin who died
young of blood-poisoning
on the cusp of fame.

She embodies his dilemma:
how to keep the music
flowing through the keyboard,
through the gliding ice;

how, from frozen embers,
to re-ignite his fire.
She gains high marks
for style, interpretation:

nimble figures flowing
through the agile minds
of shrewd adjudicators
lining the rink-side.

As she stems her flow,
on hearing loud applause
this ice-maiden melts
into a drenching smile.

HAYDN CONCERT AT VIENNA

In quiet anticipation,
we await the opening bars
of the hundredth symphony;
downbeat of the maestro's wand
holds us in the hand of silence;
themes unfold with measured tread,
violinists at the head.

No jarring note disrupts
the evenness of the score;
it echoes no inner angst,
no sense of impending chaos
in the world beyond the hall.
It is polarity of Schoenberg,
who counterpoints our strident age.

A pause suspends attention:
the first movement ends
in a shuffling of feet,
half-suppressed coughs,
a keen sense of relief that
the world is as it should be,
harmonious, sane, complete.

HANDEL'S *Messiah*

The initial composition
of this well-loved oratorio
took him only three weeks,
in a burst of creativity.

A long performance record
at the Foundlings' Hospital,
in the composer's lifetime,
prompted constant revision.

Each version was different
in some material way
from all its forerunners,
to fit in with the abilities

of available musicians
(give or take the odd sackbut),
financial constraints,
the soloists' range.

After the fourteenth season
of presenting the work,
he produced a fair copy
with his final adjustments.

It was duly bequeathed
to the hospital trustees
as part of his testament,
in the version we hear today.

JOSEPH HAYDN
(1732-1809)

He regarded himself
as akin almost to a serf
bound to the estate of
Nikolaus Esterhazy.

He was into his fifties
when the old count died
and the young heir decreed
court music obsolete.

Experiencing freedom
for the first time in his life,
he spurned local offers
and headed for London,

then the most cultured
of European centers,
rivaling in prestige
his native Vienna.

In free hours he chose
to stroll in Hyde Park;
received into society,
he was well-dined and wined.

In constant demand
as conductor or composer,
his musical stature
was belatedly recognized.

JEAN SIBELIUS: *Symphony No. 4 in A minor*

It summons to the forest depths
where ice-birds call across
a frozen, living silence;
transposing in the spring
to the high-pitched note
of piccolo, flute and oboe,
the deep, reedy tone
of the bassoon.

Forests roll upon themselves
and fold into the taiga's dense
green symphony of trees,
where woodwind call to us
from stiller worlds; skein of
wild geese flying and the cranes
is all its tenuous echo,
its undulating theme.

Breadth of lakes
extends the surface tension;
their depth is clarity of sound,
the pure awakened spring,
rippled with a leitmotif
of beating, rhythmic wings.
Storm clouds gather weight
across these waters, ominous as dreams.

INTIMATE VOICE

From Radio Finland
comes a recording
of Jean Sibelius
in his native idiom;
warm and vibrant,
his deep baritone
is graveled by age.

Voces Intimae
was written in London,
his 3rd Symphony in Paris;
one should live, he claimed,
in the heart of a city
or in the midst of a forest,
where silence reigns.

He sowed wild oats
with Helsinki cronies
in a fling of hard living,
while studying violin
as hopeful virtuoso;
then withdrew to Ainola,
his lake-forest home.

The voice of Sibelius
is more typically heard
in eloquent tone-poems
composed in the spirit
and freedom of Liszt:
evocations of nature
and of Nordic myths.

SEA SYMPHONY
(after Claude Debussy's *La Mer*)

Hauntingly is heard
over an open sea
a thin, insistent call
discovering the silence.

The urgent theme
builds majestically
on itself, swelling out
to a romantic horizon;

where its note is held,
adagio, sforzando,
in an elegant line
above the crosscurrents:

slow sirens
of the rising wind,
the adventurous lore
of off-shore rovers.

And the sea composes
a choral symphony:
all our voices,
those of its deep denizens;

the cries of mermaids
in the teeth of the gale;
of unvoiced mariners
in the throats of gulls.

ARNOLD SCHOENBERG IN AMERICA

Already a celebrity,
he quit 1930s Vienna
to escape anti-Semitism
and settled in America,
where he quickly embraced
the new way of life.

But he grew concerned,
perhaps a little irked,
when his Hollywood home
was somehow omitted
from sight-seeing tours
of the movie stars.

Maybe he assumed
that his twelve-tone system,
a revolution in music
understood by the few,
had struck a resonant chord
with the general public.

If he genuinely craved
broad popular acclaim,
it was on account of his faith
in his artistic mission:
his was to be the new,
enduring future of music.

ARNOLD SCHOENBERG: *Transfigured Night* (Opus 4)

If it has no tonal center,
what shall we hold on to
in our search for bearings,
for verities, for certainty?

Shall we accept uncertainty,
its pragmatic anguish,
as bearing more surely
on our true condition?

Or shall we, like the Viennese,
evade this uneasy truth with
the hisses, boos and ridicule
that greeted its debut?

In night's kaleidoscope,
little is predictable: all is flux,
the unstemmed flow of emotion
its lodestar, its verity.

AN EVENING WITH DAGMAR KRAUSE
(Royal Exchange Theatre, Manchester)

Hands clasped tightly,
nightly wringing
tension from the music;
flaxen hair falling
in unbraided cascade
over mobile features,
she evokes an atmosphere
of Berlin in the thirties
with Hans Eisler's songs.

Her adroit accompanist
alternates nimbly
between Bechstein grand
and jaunty accordion;
the mood swings freely
from political platform
to the comparative jollity
of Kurt Weil's popular
Threepenny Opera.

Aside from searchingly
executed set pieces,
she highlights her chosen,
pacifist composer:
aspects of his creative life
as Schoenberg's disciple;
his folksier cycle;
his asylum in America
and love affair with Hollywood.

MOZART THE MAN

Like other players
in upwardly-mobile Vienna,
among the cognoscenti,
he had an uphill struggle
against the cost of living,
the crippling rents.

Natural pride balked
at his menial treatment
by a clerical patron;
upsetting precedent,
he risked going it alone
to live by his talents.

Limited means
were meant to stretch
to fashionable clothes,
spa resorts, top schools;
to maintain appearances,
to attract commissions.

Prosecution for debt
aggravated his already
dire financial stress,
brought loss of face in
this status-conscious place;
credibility was everything.

Not *The Magic Flute*,
an overnight triumph,
nor long concert tours,
could restore his fortunes;
weakened by fever,
he succumbed to the struggle.

PERFORMING A BACH CANTATA
(Mache Dich mein Geist bereit)

Near-panic sets in
as the musicians scramble
to catch up with the start
of a rolling Bach cantata.

Like rushing to board
a crack inter-city express
as it is leaving the platform,
the conductor harrying them.

Set for a breathless run,
the chorus is firmly seated,
sober, alert, composed,
schedules spread before them.

A short way down the line,
after a headlong dash,
the tempo is briefly checked
to take on a high soprano.

Regal in sequined gown,
she is escorted to her place
in the foremost compartment,
the baritone rumbling after.

All are now well-primed
for the long, stately ride
through classic countryside.
She signals her first solo.

LEGACY OF J.S. BACH

Active to the end,
by then almost blind,
he penned from his sick-bed,
using an amanuensis,
one final, appropriate
musical offering.

His chattels comprised
instruments of the period,
violins and harpsichords
used in producing
keyboard, occasional
and choral music.

Cash stocks were held
in gold and silver coin;
banknotes (culminating in
the later hyper-inflation)
remained uninvented;
and there was real estate.

His private library,
leaning towards Divinity,
would have helped inspire
a contemplative mind
to liturgical writings
focused on Passiontide.

Even so monumental an output
suffered serious neglect,
before popular revival
one full century on,
by kindred compatriot,
young Felix Mendelssohn.

SCHUMANN AT THE KEYBOARD

He is somehow more personal,
unstrung to public taste;
no playing to the gallery
in this art for art's sake.

Inspired by introspection,
he probes a hidden seam
for clues to an identity,
counterpointing dreams.

He rejects surface brilliance
of a brave, prolific age,
the pantheon of talents,
the world across the stage.

He transposed the keyboard
to a subconscious mode:
an artistic precursor of
a Jung, perhaps, or Freud.

Confidence of tone falters,
agony of doubt remains,
up to his last, unreleased
imprisonment in mental chains.

SCENES FROM ROBERT SCHUMANN'S
Carnival (Opus 9)

PIERROT

He performs like a puppet,
in short jerky motions,
with slow deliberation
and a hint of pathos;
this sad, wistful figure
more readily fetches tears
than peals of laughter.

ESTRELLA

Her brief dance routine
has the consummate grace
and skill of a ballerina;
a tender, alluring display
of artistry and beauty,
with hints of the subtler
feminine mysteries.

BUTTERFLIES

Brilliant, restive spirits
on the fairground fringes,
evoking depth of summer;
fine taffeta wings beat
to their own inner rhythm,
pianissimo their music
amid the palpable din.

CHOPIN

He puts in a brief appearance
as celebrity virtuoso,
his performance at once
romantic and restrained;
the famous composer
has strayed, or been spirited,
into this reveler's world.

FRANZ SCHUBERT
(1797-1828)

When opening a theme,
he meant to develop it
to its fullest potential,
extending it, modulating,
transposing the key,
re-stating, recapitulating.

He seemed able to live
well inside the music,
elaborating from within
like some master-builder
constructing an edifice
sparingly about him.

As with song cycles like
Die Schone Mullerin,
so too with briefer pieces
he profusely conceived,
there is simplicity of form,
artistic completeness.

A native of Vienna,
he strolled in her woods,
responding to the poetry
of Goethe and Mayerhofer,
to launch a new art-form,
the redoubtable lied.

Fame came, but not fortune:
he eked out a spare living
from royalties and tuition,
achieving the luxury
in the last year of his life
of owning his own piano.

LATE BEETHOVEN

Having played and scored
movements, voices, chords
over a broad portfolio,
it could be said, off the record,
that the composer heard
the gamut of musical sounds,
keyed all known harmonies.

Heard himself out, in a way,
before finally descending
into that toneless world
where hearing did not serve
the compelling creativity
of his great evening period,
the years of the late quartets.

He internalized the work
inside the choir of his mind,
as in some Gothic minster
swelling voice and organ:
a veritable *Missa Solennis*
behind sealed oaken doors,
not a sound leaking out.

FREDERIC CHOPIN: *Nocturnes*

Expressive salon pieces,
they were composed
for musical soirees
when night draws in
elfin and mysterious;
les invités sit audibly still,
like statue groups
at Musée des Beaux Arts.

Tempo rubato (stolen time)
lets the performer's emotion
steal over the keyboard
and assert its own pace;
a melancholy drift
conveys pain of loss,
of parting, nostalgia,
some fresh *tristesse*.

Yet some of them set
a quite different tone,
assertive and defiant
with a marked *agitato*;
wresting us clear
of mere introspection,
scotching any suggestion
of the too-sentimental.

KAROL SZYMANOWSKI
(1882-1937)

Unlike Mozart,
who by his best efforts
could not escape poverty,
this composer chose it,
rejecting offers elsewhere
to be adamantly there.

He sought a native style
based on the regional
folk songs of Poland
and the Tatra Mountains;
much as Bela Bartok
harmonized Hungary.

After the Great War,
there was a vacuum to fill
in the cultural identity
of this liberated state;
taste had long centered
on the court at Vienna.

Not since Chopin,
who remained an émigré,
had Poland seen a musical
hero; scoring abroad,
but neglected at home,
he received meager reward.

AULIS SALINEN: *Symphony No. 3* (The Sea)

It propels itself,
endlessly powered
by a restless energy
holding off-shore.

Surface is stormy;
gulls, petrels
skim in proximity
to lifting waves.

A brief calm follows;
eerie, as the sea,
impending, spreads out
in still expectancy.

From unfettered depths
anything may arise:
blue whale, oceanid,
Polaris, wreckage.

The waves re-agitate,
as at the passage
of some grand armada
anticipating battle.

The neutral sea
now heaves in sympathy,
in a kind of synergy
with cleaving keels.

MALE VOICE CHOIR

A well-tuned platoon,
they troop onto the stage,
heads held sentry-erect,
composing stray features,
the hair's loose strand.

Soon into the taxing score
voices from a depth arise,
the young with the very old
peering through half-lenses
with defensive eyes.

Uniformity of dress masks
each his sterner calling:
a lawyer with no brief,
a seer now unseen,
revealing Elgar's Dream.

The pathos of the music,
its elegaic song, masks
for each a personal grief
that slowly bleeds within him,
a deep, unsounded stream.

IOLANTHE AT GAWSWORTH HALL

As prelude to evening's
open-air performance,
the tour of private rooms
highlights family history
in portraits on the walls.

The Cheshire landscape
dreams beyond the hall,
distanced in generations
from its key Royalist role
in the English Civil War.

Lights from leaded widows
overlook the tailored lawns,
hollyhocks, boxed hedges,
blending domesticity
with fantasy of form.

An enchanted world emerges
from the faerie darkness,
as doting English law lords
dance enigmatic rings
round Chancery's fair ward.

PUBLIC ART GALLERY

It stands on a busy corner
of the square; the uncurious
stroll past rotating doors,
the fixed commissionaire.

A few will step inside;
the rest hang it like a picture
on the wall of the main street,
collecting atmospheric dust.

It takes some moral effort
to go in, to face up squarely
to so much mere perfection
assembled in a single place.

We may even feel ourselves
somehow unworthy to countenance
such beauty; from a sense
of trespass hurry on outside,

feeling a sudden strong relief,
hitting us with the city air,
that we are once more excused
a searching self-examination.

JAN VAN EYCK: *The Arnolfini Wedding*

The gown might then be emerald,
like the one the bride is wearing
clasping her new husband's hand.

The groom cocks a stovepipe hat
above a long vermilion smock,
his unengaged right palm

raised as if in salutation,
or to invoke a blessing on
this solemn nuptial scene

for true domestic harmony,
increase, health in what may be
a financier's rich milieu.

It was a time in Europe
when they equipped interiors
with fine art and furnishings

like the gilt chandelier
and the sturdy double bed
draped in conspicuous red.

Can we really conjure now
who these Arnolfinis were;
what sudden, unexpected rifts

dented their wedded bliss?
All now seems fair set,
cloudless; issue to beget.

ALBRECHT DUERER: *Adam and Eve*

Duerer's Adam is a tall,
lean, athletic man
who would compete well
at a modern pentathlon;
tilting slightly forward
on the ball of his foot,
he looks poised for action
as springboard of mankind.
A sense of genuine wonder
plays about clear eyes,
not at the outside world,
at finding himself alive.

Eve is serenely featured
taking an early stroll
amid the apple groves;
her left hand reaches out
discerning the way ahead,
finding a path through Time.
This engaging female
has hues of the olive south
playing about her skin,
dancing around her mouth;
one for the Lido beaches
soon as the sun comes out.

PIETER BRUEGHEL: *Tower of Babel*

Looms a vast citadel,
turrets wreathed in cloud,
base crowding the plain.

Different tiers present
barriers in communication
too steep to surmount;

or ever more rarified
levels of consciousness
separating people out.

Siege-towers and ladders
are positioned to assail
less accessible places:

the tendency men have
to misunderstand each other,
to misinterpret words.

Figures wandering about
in search of meaning
look vaguely disoriented.

And on the battlements
a heavy cannon is mounted
to shoot off at the mouth.

PIETER BRUEGHEL: *Death of the Virgin*

In an inglenook the maid,
tired from her ministrations,
dozes unceremoniously
by the roaring fire.

She remains oblivious
of the voiceless keeners
harmoniously stealing
to the pale bedside.

They tail back endlessly
into the Orient night,
from limbos of antiquity
entering the light.

Eager to press forward
as due decorum allows;
to be all of mankind
at the borders of Time;

to be tenderly present
at this momentous event,
and take a vital part
of a flawless parting.

PIETER BRUEGHEL:
Massacre of the Innocents

The scene is translated
from Herodian Judaea
to winter in Flanders.

White slanted roofs,
squat village dwellings,
the overcast sky

and deep-frozen river
do not readily suggest
blood, heat and dust,

wailing of infants seized,
anguish of mothers,
paroxysms of grief.

Emotions are blanketed
under a pall of snow
softening dealt blows.

In this chilling scene,
the helmeted phalange
brandishing lances

is about to set out
on its heartless enterprise:
gratuitous infanticide.

JACOPO de BARBARI:
Portrait of Luca Pacioli

The commanding Franciscan
objectively deduces,
for university students,
the beauties of Euclid.

A gifted mathematician,
his studies in perspective
helped his friend Leonardo
arrange *The Last Supper.*

Close by him, his shadow,
stands a young Venetian
elegantly representing
the style of the Quattrocento.

This Luca helped foster
through versatile contacts
with artists and scholars
descending on Florence.

Taut, ascetic features
attest knowledge as truth;
that it is vision and life
is confirmed by the youth.

CARAVAGGIO: *Conversion of St. Paul*

In this dramatic incident
on the road to Damascus,
Saul is thrown from the saddle.

Lying flat on his back,
he appears to be hearkening
to a voice from the clouds.

His steed stands testily
over him, as if scenting
a sudden change in the wind,

a new and different agenda
from the fury of the chase,
the hounding of believers,

snatched stabling and sleep;
to the relentless attrition
of missionary journeys.

Saul's loyal manservant,
his brow deeply furrowed,
attempts to steady the beast.

Is he *really* witnessing
this extraordinary scene
unfolding before him?

His defining moment, too:
instant redeployment,
from henchman to disciple.

BOCCACCIO BOCCACCINO: *Gypsy Girl*

She has wide blue eyes,
this traveler's daughter,
full of fine intelligence
that will not have come
from formal education,
but in the school of life
as it surprises on the road.

A blue checkered kerchief
tightly knotted to one side
frames a pale oval face;
tresses descend unchecked,
part-hidden down her neck,
lending an air of modesty
blending with her simple dress.

No hint of a girlish smile
plays about her mouth;
red lips remain tight-set,
her appealing demeanor
is guarded, worldly-wise;
mistrusting, one might find,
of the foibles of mankind.

PETER PAUL RUBENS:
Descent from the Cross

Perhaps only this master
could successfully invest
such immanence of death
with insistent rhythm.

Clambering agilely on
well-propped ladders,
men bend almost double
over the rude crosstree

to lower the body down,
linking hand over hand
in a pastoral symphony
of synchronized movement.

Sturdy, concerted limbs
and taut, engrossed features
contrast in tone and color
with the wan, limp figure

descending heavily
into loving arms receiving,
indeed already sizing
the long white winding shroud.

PETER PAUL RUBENS: *The Village Wedding*

The scene is a sunlit day
at the rustic village edge,
by undulating countryside,
a stream with tufts of sedge.

The village wedding dance
is a wild high-jinks affair;
the guests link up and fling
bare limbs into the air.

No set quadrilles here;
raw energy and pace
make up for what is lacking
in etiquette and grace.

Couples in a long embrace
clinch tightly, roll about;
romance is infectious,
it will have its day out.

Kinship groups are seated
at ease upon the grass,
punctuating eager speech
with gesturing and laughs.

The quiet one is the infant
plugged to his mother's breast;
or the swain with flagon drained
of mead, or is it stout?

WILLIAM HOGARTH: *The Painter's Servants*

Well presented, they gaze
out on the Enlightenment
with an air of purpose,
sobriety and contentment.

Not one of the six,
evenly split by gender,
ranging widely in age,
wears the trace of a smile.

Perhaps life below stairs
was unremittingly grim,
even in the household
of a celebrated satirist.

Or a smile may be hard
to capture on canvas;
which is why *Mona Lisa*
is intriguingly unique.

That these lowly folk,
who did not have the vote,
should be posing at all
for a formal group portrait

speaks of an artist with
the true common touch,
a genuine egalitarian
in a class-conscious age.

MEINDERT HOBBEMA: *The Avenue, Middleharnis*

Piled high with clouds,
the sky is tinged vermilion
pending an autumn storm.

Cumulus cap the crowns
of poplars standing sentry
like impassive palace guards.

Wind-twisted either hand,
there's a gap or two where
a sudden gale broke through.

The low-lying polder,
well-husbanded, flows on
to where the rising spire

of a distant village,
red-roofed, deep in tillage,
peals a clear diapason.

Rutted, caked in mud,
the going gets tough in winter,
open to frost and flood.

FRANCESCO GUARDI:
Feast of the Ascension at Venice

They take to the lagoon
in all conceivable craft,
ensigns gaily flying
from tall, spare masts.

This water-city rose
from islands in the bay
settled by refugees
fleeing Attila the Hun.

Hailing each other then
with a thankful *Veni etiam*
(I came this far), they
coined the name Venezia.

What more fitting way
for watermen to celebrate,
affluent centuries on,
the rising of the Son?

This proud city-state,
riding the swell of trade,
liked to reminisce upon
achievements of famous men:

her acclaimed painters
Titian, Canaletto, Tiepolo;
merchants, financiers, doges
and adventurer Marco Polo.

THE IMPRESSIONISTS

They rediscovered landscape,
fixing the mobility of nature,
its constant flux and change,
under light's shifting play.

Nature was not for them
something still and static,
as backcloth for a portrait,
formal, ordered, tame.

They took precise moments
in time, sought out weather;
to paint, say, in a snowstorm
enhanced the impression.

Quitting the studio,
its devices and stereotypes,
they made for the outdoors,
the common scenes of life:

the lie of city streets,
steam railways, riversides;
cafes, theatres, cabarets,
the rhythms of the everyday.

Theirs was the fluid world
of Claude Debussy's music;
of *Reflets dans l'Eau*
and *Jardins sous la Pluie*.

CLAUDE MONET: *Gare St-Lazare*

Dense clouds of steam
conspire to lend the scene
ethereality, like a kind

of thin gauze veil through
which one may discern
outlines of material things;

like the Paris tenements
just dimly visible
in the station precincts.

A vintage locomotive
shunts slowly into view
beneath the vaulted roof.

Impassive human figures
lurk just off-center
in a loose, sporadic group.

Unencumbered with luggage,
they give a vague impression
of waiting for a train.

VINCENT van GOGH: *Sunflowers*

Each is a radiant sun
in its own right,
against a backdrop
of clear yellow light;

configured here,
with green haloes,
in the burnt sienna
of Provencal afternoons.

No bird sojourns;
no cloud absorbs
the liquid glare
of the meridian.

These fierce suns
blaze out on us
from strangely artless,
uncosmetic faces;

with a wholly sensuous,
cosmic kind of energy
spiking the roots
of complacency.

EDVARD MUNCH: *Madonna*

Up she comes drifting
out of the maelstrom
in the Norwegian Sea,
naked arms whirling,
raven hair swirling
in long epaulettes
over sea-wet breasts.

Her ship-wrecked,
pale and watery torso
ignites a stark desire;
sea-nymph singing
by submerged rocks
draws men swiftly down
in a drowning spiral.

This is no Madonna
of the theater boards,
a siren for our time;
but the untamed libido
of a repressed age
struggling to surface,
to liberate, to rage.

IGOR GRABAR: *Morning Tea. Snowdrops*

A gleaming samovar
dominates a corner of the table,
offsetting the rosewood dresser.

Tea has been poured,
a few comestibles spread out
across the soft linen cloth.

Most tempting of these,
fresh peaches and a wedge
of pure goat's-milk cheese.

Though no one is yet down,
we already know a lot
about the rousing occupants:

their passion for order,
the ideal of the rustic life
lived to its highest values;

contentment in simplicity,
and a hint of that rude health
enjoyed amid mountains.

Altitude snowdrops grow,
to fill the porcelain bowl
hailing this simple feast.

At almost any moment
the early riser will appear,
regaled by scent and color.

ANTONI GAUDI: *Casa Mila* (Barcelona)

Vegetal in conception,
like his famous cathedral,
the Sagrada Familia,
it extends metal tendrils
across window balconies.

Sun-tanned Catalans
dwell behind drawn blinds
designed to resemble
swollen seedpods.
Do they feel closer to nature

in these shaded living-spaces,
a sense of harmony
with their environment,
an inner peace? Or are they
just as testy as the rest?

Here is an attempt to
circumvent the alienation
of modern urban life;
to cross a vital border,
through architectural form,

between a rootless
and a natural lifestyle;
to create a leafy enclave
in the midst of a city,
in a modern apartment block.

ART NOUVEAU

Decorative artists,
heirs of William Morris,
instigated a movement
against mass production.

Their aim was to create
useful everyday objects
(vases, lamps, chairs)
inspired by natural forms.

Plants, birds, sea-shells
became motifs for wares
to restore city-dwellers
to a more vital environment

and deliver the artisan
from his workaday world,
from the toxins and grime
of an industrial milieu.

Their expert craftsmanship,
investing skill and time,
could not compete for cost
with modern assembly-lines.

Although it spread widely
in the wake of industrialism,
this 'art for all' faltered,
an inspired ideal declined.

CUBISM

In representational art,
ancient as cavemen,
the subject is central.

After Darwin and Jung
that place gave way
to broader perspectives.

Evolutionists slip us
into a stream of life
from the primordial slime.

The depths of the mind
contain racial memories,
shared annals of time.

Cubists aimed to portray
these multiple facets
of our complex identity.

Chagall, for example,
in *I and the Village*,
combines Russian folklore

with Jewish proverbs,
up-country scenes,
robust peasant life.

If such art is unsettling,
it may be from uncertainty
about who we really are.

UMBERTO BOCCIONI:
The Noise of the Street enters the House (1911)

A fair invades the town;
barrel-organ music vies
with motley local chimes,
piercing the summer night
with sharp staccato vibes.

St. Januarius is chaired
down a narrow Naples street;
the faithful stand three-deep,
chant and cry. For why?
His blood had liquefied.

Blood runs in tumbrels
through Place du Caroussel;
the Old Regime is laid
at the whetting of a blade.
They sing the *Marseillaise.*

The sound of shattering
plate glass is heard
on Kristallnacht; the breath
of violence fills the air,
the jackboot mounts the stair.

JEAN ARP: *Torso* (1931)

The marble gleams
like a living body
oiled, toned, bronzed.

Even shorn of limbs,
it preserves the rhythms
of an agile man,

as practiced gymnast
clinging to a beam,
slowly levering;

or athlete poised
to throw a discuss,
launch a javelin.

Beauty lies in curves
as they slide down
this tensile stone

in unbroken motion,
from shoulder blades
through arc of back.

Classic pentathlon
seen as human ideal;
man as superman.

GIORGIO DI CHIRICO:
Grand Metaphysician (1917)

Most intriguing is
the gaping pedal-bin
placed at the base
of the sculpture's plinth
on a piazza framed
by classical arcades.

The metaphysician
sits atop an assortment
of technical objects:
theodolite, quadrant,
orb, tripod that might
somehow assist a seer.

That bin. An ideal world
will cater for waste,
a liberal by-product
of our consumer society:
leavings, litter, lees,
dross, refuse, debris.

Metaphysical concepts
might include recycling,
re-use of consumer durables;
the aesthetic effect
of a tidy environment,
of pollution-free zones.

JOHN ROLAND BARKER:
Fishing Boats in the Harbour, Mevagissy

With its quintessential
lime-washed cottages,
fronting the raucous quay
teeming with seagulls,
Mevagissy seems to be
in thrall to the swirling sea.

As if the waves imposed
their contours on the land,
as on strong fishing hulls
with sturdy, curved timbers
well-built to withstand
whatever the rollers hand.

Cobbled streets wind steeply
down to the spreading sea,
where sharp-eyed gulls
crowd the mackerel smacks
off-loading a recent catch,
to claim their mendicant share.

JOHN MARIN: *Singer Building* (1921)

A feeling here for the beat
of the commercial heart
of the city, its innocence
before the Wall Street Crash.

An inkling too of the chaos
inherent in the ruthless
pursuit of pecuniary gain
and competitive edge.

The stark skyscraper
seems about to launch itself
from its fixed moorings,
as if high aspirations,

for profit or for status,
cannot be circumscribed
by the staid parameters
of the known business world:

the regulated beat, say,
of Threadneedle Street;
the polychromatic rhythms
of London's Petticoat Lane.

It portrays the apotheosis
of the business corporation,
the elevation of liberalism
to a continental creed.

WILLEM de KOONING: *Woman*

Plenty of flesh and blood
in this unblushing abstract;
very little resembling
the conventional feminine:
no pout of lips, smile,
hour-glass figure, style.

Copious reds suggest
warmth of feeling, blood
lilting through young veins,
the maternal instinct, love;
carmine lipstick, rouge
become the pure seducer.

Yet other primary colors
conjure printed fabrics
chosen in all their gaiety
to suit indulgent summer;
swatch of green is Nature
basking in her sea of fields.

EDWARD HOPPER: *Rooms by the Sea*

The front door stands open,
to let directly on the sea;
unlocked waves drift away
to the powder-blue horizon.

A shaft of bright sunlight
flows across the threshold,
gripping the bare room
in an intense yellow glow.

One half expects to find
someone framed in that space,
about to plunge into sheer sea;
or a spinnaker skim by.

The second, inner room
has spartan red furniture ;
arranged, it stands waiting
in the stalled morning hour.

Has the tenant slipped out
for a moment, or gone for aye?
Are these sea rooms vacant
pending summer occupation?

EDWARD HOPPER: *Yawl Riding a Swell*

Long off Cape Cod,
the boat sails solo;
tacks across banks
of the North Atlantic.

Out on the blue light
a squall whips up;
wind grips the waves,
which lift and lave.

The yawl holds steady,
undeterred, unswayed;
white sails fake
the sky's smudged pearl.

A strong hull plays
on the celeste of the sea;
light-blue on a blue,
but the sea prevails.

The two-man crew
ride high in the stern;
as fore and aft
wild sea-pipes skirl.

EDWARD HOPPER:
New York Movie (1939)

Quite a plush place,
your city movie theatre;
patrons settle deep
in damask armchairs,
absorbing atmosphere.

Aside, there is a gap
in velvet curtains leading
to approaching stairs;
no one's entry is expected,
to distract or to disturb.

The usherette stands stiffly
in a lilac evening gown;
she has an absent air,
screening her own thoughts
beneath Garbo hair.

The action of the film
is not her main concern;
her fixed gaze is averted,
the drama is internal,
projecting solely onto her.

EDWARD HOPPER: *Dories, Ogunquit*

Sea was never so blue
as the deeps off Ogunquit;
rocks were rarely so red
as the inshore rocks.

The dories string out
across an unsheltered bay,
in a loose-enough queue
with maneuvering room.

Fishermen are long gone,
up onto the lonely land,
waiting on patient wives
between opulent tides.

Boats were never so white
as these anchored smacks;
unmasted, without sheets,
they ride ghost-like.

EDWARD HOPPER: *Nighthawks* (1942)

Loneliness stares in
through the picture windows
of this all-night diner,
conveying its aura
across deserted sidewalks;
uninviting, yet inviting
to the brightness of its bar.

The trio clientele
sit in silence waiting,
perhaps not waiting,
for someone to communicate;
to break the monotony
of long night-vigils,
of the unaffected cigarette.

Rooted to high stools,
they do not appear
to have come from anywhere,
nor to be on their way;
but to have materialized
out of the cold precinct,
off endless thoroughfares.

SALVADOR DALI: *Crucifixion*

The cross is raised
over a surreal landscape,
its taut figure, head bowed,
arms spread-eagled,
like a giant bird looks down
upon a new dawn breaking
over a calm inland sea,
which could be Galilee.

On the shore, a barque
is waiting for a navigator;
for the next solo voyager
into uncharted waters,
the spiritual unknown,
its swirling currents,
unplumbed depths
and hidden reefs.

The fisherman standing
at the tide's edge
casting his net wide
seems truly diminutive
in the overall figuring:
an image of mankind
in the shadow of the cross,
in the valleys of Time.

L.S. LOWRY: *Going to the Match*

First impressions are
of a faceless mass
of soccer fans pressing,
almost uniform in step,
towards the ballpark;
the backdrop is of cotton mills
with tall smoking stacks.

Each matchstick man
is yet a rounded individual
lovingly depicted in
all his eccentricity,
style of dress and gait;
distinct from the crowd,
yet sharing mental space.

Stoically independent
in his approach to life,
he knows all worth knowing
from his own rain-swept perspective;
like the Salford artist himself,
he has a unique, wry,
inimitable style.

REGARDING AN ICON

If it lacks perspective,
it's because that technique,
pending a Leonardo,
had not yet been invented.

Lines do not converge
to vanishing point; they travel
on beyond the picture,
seeking out infinity.

Archangel Michael stands
girding his authentic might,
red-caped, wings draped,
heavy breastplate weightless.

His eyes do not invite
our due return of gaze,
nor do they clearly focus;
their import is unspoken.

Sword is free of scabbard,
keen-edged, held aloft,
its bearer at the sharp end
of the war in heaven.

SELF-PORTRAIT

Early portrait painters
fulfilled commissions
from prominent patrons
canvassing spent years.

Self-portraiture came later,
as the artist found himself
equal in human worth
to his worldlier peers.

It mirrored the break-up
of hierarchical societies
based on class and rank;
enter the self-made man.

Freud speeded the process;
by exposing our neuroses,
he found a shared humanity
beneath the old veneers.

A logical extension
is modern autobiography:
subjects from all walks of life
on their own literary canvas.

AMERICAN FILM

It opens in cinemascope,
with an armchair view
of the burning road;
enter an automobile,
truck or mobile home.

Since the first caravans
made the yearning west,
some have kept going
(when long settled down),
opening Cumberland Gap
in the back of the mind.

The end of the road is
innocent beginning,
a real estate killing;
a run for the border
and beyond to Sonora;
an excuse-me slow dance,
a hi-jacked romance.

There is extended metaphor
for infinity of spirit,
through a Mojave Desert
of wandering being;
our cactus isolation,
which still prickles when
the highway re-enters
the slick of the city.

WATCHING CHARLIE CHAPLIN

His silent films speak volumes
on the turmoil in ourselves:
how the last strand of happiness
eludes us from the elaborate
web we weave to capture it.

And the desire to preserve
the whole world our familiar
childhood playground; to peep
round the edges of reality
without actually glimpsing it.

To shun the harsher truths,
defer the coming of adulthood;
awareness of good and evil;
the need to define our true
position this side of Eden.

Through all this there is
the childlike falling in love,
which alone can be the anodyne
to the pathos of our lives;
which alone redeems everything.

MARILYN MONROE

From hapless orphan,
she transformed herself,
with Hollywood's help,
into the stuff of dreams,
the original sex symbol.

Many men, it is said,
in female relationships
are seeking another mother,
to cater to their psychic
and material needs.

Marilyn aimed to appeal
to more basic instincts,
to illustrate the theme
common to all romantic
novels, songs and films.

'Boy meets girl' became
a recurring key motif
of her screen career;
more so of her private life,
in high-profile marriages.

What all this amounts to,
when the music subsides,
the final curtain falls,
the patrons quit the stalls,
is replication of one's genes.

AUGUST STRINDBERG
(1849-1912)

With his young bride Frieda
the flamboyant dramatist
entrained for Heligoland
to by-pass wedding banns.

He hugged a portmanteau
with his novel-in-progress
and manuscripts of plays
destined for the German stage.

His original theories
on a range of scientific data,
including even alchemy,
tumbled in on scraps of paper.

Laboratory equipment
(what honeymoon experiments
did he have in mind?) was alone
entrusted to the luggage van.

Dramatic oil paintings,
too bulky to accompany them,
were all he left behind
in safe storage in Berlin.

But marriage did not settle
this widely-scattered man,
with bits in major cities;
with Delius, Munch, Gauguin.

SWEDISH FILM

It resembles a goldfish
outside of the bowl,
peering in on itself
through oblique lenses.

Each movement is noted,
analyzed, dissected:
why does it swim this way,
or that? Why swim at all?

The other goldfish: why
do they act as they do,
swimming past each other
in apparent oblivion?

One suddenly stops,
its mouth drops open;
for air bubbles it emits
a soliloquy on life.

With studied slowness
and precision of speech,
it utters some subtle,
sunken profundity.

In the swirling depths
of this hermetic world,
one can still faintly hear
Edvard Munch's *Scream*.

WILFRID OWEN (d. 1918):
Anthem for Doomed Youth

Engaging, that his temperament
could formulate these words
in the teeth of heavy guns
on the unquiet Western Front;
unknowingly (and movingly)
he was evoking his own demise
amid the vibrancy of life.

Not even dire conditions,
the hell of trench warfare,
could quench the ever-kindling
fires of his creative mind;
as if he stood outside events,
viewing them objectively,
with unique detachment.

A poem may be the most
cogent of the spirit's vital signs;
that which contrasts starkly
with the pitiless reduction
of the battlefield; token of
the unyielding life of the mind
faced with near-certain death.

POETRY ANTHOLOGY

Eclectic in scope,
this assemblage of authors
highlights key insights
and existential delights.

While some died young,
most lived long lives,
to keep ideas flowing,
a seed within them growing

slowly, subconsciously,
to blossom forth a poem;
as exhibition tea roses
half a lifetime sowing.

Here we see them grafted
onto one artificial stem:
scented petals of the mind
variegated, yet of a kind.

In life they may have been
quite hostile to each other;
avid individualists seldom,
if ever, bound together.

WALLACE STEVENS AT HARTFORD
(1916-1955)

A dedicated lawyer
in the insurance industry,
he negotiated claims;
revered by his colleagues
for his intellect and wit,
yet aloof, a famous name.

Foregoing a motor car,
he strolled to the office
through Elizabeth Park,
to sharpen his faculties,
finding thirteen ways
of looking at a blackbird.

One of the boys socially,
he loved club lunches
and ritual fishing trips
south to the Florida Keys,
engaging colors, moods,
the surreal of the sea.

Claims business in New York
was an excuse to visit
art galleries, bookstores;
to order wines and cultivate
the broad, epicurean side
of his prolific double life.

MISCELLANY

BOYHOOD

Running wild, with free
unfettered footsteps in the park,
he climbs into a northern oak
yielding, from strewn wreckage,
the acorn of a viable idea.

He renounces no ambition:
one day he may be anything
his urgent heart desires:
an astronaut, something apart
from the common race of men.

Time, which arrives slowly,
may only be a learning process
in the art of renunciation;
of a gradual, phased retreat
from the walls of innocence.

Of eventually being asked,
with quiet, immense authority,
freely to leave the park.
Or is this private realm a garden?
Is its real name is Eden?

VISITING THE OLD SCHOOL

Venerable it is. Ivy clings
to its hermetic porch sealing
out the uninvited, those who
have no daily business there;
welcoming only familiars,
who treat with affectations
of disdain the years they went
in awe of Grimes and plagued
his more well-meaning friends.

A gasp of breath as we attain
the inner sanctum of despair.
Quickly exhaled: it is half-term,
only contract cleaners there
sweeping alluvial dust and chalk,
the cobwebs of the mind.

Past glass-partitioned rooms
are glimpsed through open doors
deserted desks accustomed
to so much of adolescent life,
the fading legends etched
on the intimate insides of lids.

So much drama too, it eked
into the walls and fabric,
to linger with the ghosts
of breathless childhood,
as with those of friends
whose future lives declined
to mingle freely with one's own;
who moved to other towns,
took different jobs, got wed,
pursued careers abroad.

THE FRENCH TEACHER

Like St. Francis he was gentle;
he would talk to birds in the
park abutting the high school
in that tense quarter of the town,
and of the knowing innocence
of adolescent girls and boys.

He had learned the viciousness
of life lived at the knife's edge
on military service in the desert:
man's strife and the sanded
secrets of his soul as they unfold
beneath the tolling stars.

But did not reck the hidden fang
within the hearts of half-hewn men,
holding them in the tenderness
meant for fragile growing things;
not in the stern, affirming hand
that bends them to the rule.

THE UPPER ROOM

The upper room awaits;
a lamp flickers moth-like
on the still piano by the wall,
echoing its arbitrary silence.

The atmosphere expects;
for each a place is set
within the dimmed intimacy
reaching out towards the stairs.

The corner clock ticks thinly,
like the fainter heart-beat
that will soon wear out
the hours of patient waiting.

Silver has been polished,
and the wine decanter stands
filled with a deep bouquet
beside a vase of fading flowers.

The window stands part-open
on the softer evening air,
above the thinning noise of streets
when shadows re-appear.

MODERN ARTIFACTS

Short on human input,
on craftsmanship, on art,
they are reeled off by robots
on primed assembly lines.

Investing little, we get
little in return: a mere utility,
soon upstaged by something
just as useful, as facile.

A Guarnerius is different:
we love its purity of style;
feel, in the tone of the wood,
a quickening of pulse, a charm.

It is played for centuries,
tuning to the truth of a past
whose common objects—
a vase, a chair—were *objets d'art*.

And as we mass-produce,
our values waltz apart;
the system clones more robots,
with no conscience, no heart.

MISERICORD

In the monastic routine
of prayer, work, fasting,
each waking hour filled
to crowd out temptation,
concessions were made
to frail human nature;
a relaxation of the rule,
some pity in the heart
(*miseri cordis*)
for the weaker brethren
or the sick, who could
regale themselves betimes
on a good tonic wine.

To that end, no doubt,
the great foundations
distilled fine liqueurs
(Chartreuse, Benedictine)
not solely for the trade;
to pre-empt the Tempter.

If then a dispensation,
it could also be a ledge
on the upturned seat
of a carved choir stall,
to support the posterior
when routinely required
to remain upright during
the long canonical hours
of vespers, matins, lauds.

THE MAKER'S SONG

We are groping blindly
in the dark, with both hands,
across the skin surface of things,
reaching for the hidden unity
behind appearances.

We are groping blindly
in the light, with both hands,
across the skin surface of each other,
reaching for the ultimate union,
beyond orgasm.

The artist is groping,
in the light and in the dark,
to draw together the warring
elements of experience, forging
a new unity, with new heart;

to include elements of a brute reality,
the evil, the suffering, the squalor
that are dimensions of disunity;
drawing them back into a Whole,
redeeming them through art.

HOLE

For an empty space,
it has tremendous weight.

Calcutta's was black,
an enclave of squalor.

In a modern warship,
it sinks bottomless dollars.

An argument with one
is similarly crippled.

Manholes are chauvinist,
they don't admit women.

The pigeon's affords us
a way to procrastinate.

Some holes we get in,
we may never get out.

Ominous black ones
lurk in the universe.

The nineteenth must be
by far the most welcoming.

FREEZER COD

When he heaved it from the slab,
clinging ice and trailing blood,
and tossed on the waiting scale,
I marveled at its dappled trunk,
its firm and ocean-threshing tail
that steered it till quite recently
through the frigid Arctic seas,
the high-Atlantic swell.

Along its silver, tensile flank,
supple as the flexing tide,
were yellow, blue and green
markings in a mottled stream;
slick of blood, a dorsal fin
rising up from rigid spine;
across the unswabbed counter,
a pungent whiff of brine.

The coldly-heaving seas
are just raw eating-places,
unlicensed sushi bars;
unknown creatures thrive,
prey and predator survive;
placed in a themed marine,
fed each day but hardly dined,
the killer whale begins to die.

QUAYSIDE MACKEREL

The blood-soaked puddle of its eye
drew me into sightless depths
across the marbled contours
of its spine, burnished, dapple-dark,
defined above a pallid waterline.

Its other eye was clear and calm,
with a dun, resigning look
which did not balk the sudden fate
that froze it in this nerveless state
between still-life and death;
as in the meek and wounded chine
of a dry and down-curved mouth
tight-set beside arrested gills.

Eyes that scanned the blindness
of the seas, that read the legends
of Atlantis with a deep indifference,
evade our strangely mangled world
wrung out between the holes
that bind the cords displacing
its augmented weight in air.

COELACANTH

Heirs to an ancient line
descending unmodified
from the time of dinosaurs,
it was undignified enough
for us to be recognized
on a primitive handcart
trundling to market.

Intolerable to find
our future jeopardized
from an unthinkable
source: rank over-fishing
to extract from our spine
fluids some people claim
prolong human life.

Would that our species
had not been identified!
Undiscovered, unknown,
we could peacefully roam
the south seas our home;
while the hapless shark
is sought for one valued part.

WHALES CALLING

We take sonar soundings
across the wide ocean:
six of us transmitting,
long before Marconi
secured his toe-hold,
encompassed the globe.

We clearly distinguish
clan from blue clan
with our tribal songs,
our oceanic folklore;
we acknowledge no foes
in the seas of our home.

Our pearled oyster
is the world we roam,
more sea than shell;
shepherds of the sea,
we graze its deep pastures
and sink oxygen wells.

Gone are the days
when you used our oil
to lighten and brighten
your benighted streets;
or our very bones
to make corset stays

to provide an uplift,
since sublimated into
whale-watch expeditions
from the self-same ports
that once equipped
full-rigged whaling ships.

ELEPHANTS

When they amble across
sun-blanched remains
of one of their kind
lying in the dust, elephants
(in a type of field autopsy)
probe them closely
with their trunks.

It's the massive skull
which chiefly draws them;
as the blind identify
by tracing facial features,
pachyderms discern,
by acute sense of touch,
dead members of the herd.

And they never forget:
they have memory banks
storing data about trails,
watering places, vegetation;
they even move old bones
to a more secluded spot:
thoughtful undertaking.

HIGH FLYERS

Not all the dinosaurs
were wiped out by cataclysm;
some had taken to the air
to become, with time,
as diminutive as sparrows.

Raptors such as eagles,
kites, hawks and falcons
may be distant descendants
of those early predators
with jaws for rending flesh.

Such humbler species
as visit suburban gardens
feeding on seeds and berries
could stem from herbivores
grazing Jurassic shores.

They soon took to flight,
flapping feathered limbs
to gather speed, outflank attack;
taking off from time's runway,
they never looked back.

ADAM AND EVE

An intriguing new species
emerged from the shade
of the eastward garden,
having tasted the fruit
of the knowledge tree;
paradise was for the birds,
and for living-in fools.

Behind them trailed
the roots of another tree,
the Tree of Life;
it was morally blind,
as of a mole tunneling
in the crumbling earth,
or a lumbering dinosaur.

Their brave new world
was one of polarities:
heat and cold, plenty and want,
happiness and sorrow.
They knew good from evil;
each step they now took
led to moral dilemmas.

EVERYMAN AS ODYSSEUS

He ventures out to the poles
of existence, fearful as mariners
under Columbus, viewing earth
as flat, forever turning back
on the sea of the mind.

His life's voyage is internal,
on uncharted seas of awareness,
towards the limits of experience,
cast off from the circling shore,
the womb's safe anchorage.

He drifts tide-bound and alone
on his frail, submersible craft,
on the gray vastness of ocean
that daily defines his vision,
the subconscious its hidden depth;

that which plots his course,
under-towing his reason;
that buoys him up on the sea-swell
of his own Being, even as
it threatens to overwhelm him.

MORGENLIED

Whether of flesh or clay
it matters little: I shall
diminish daily and decay.
Putrefacio, ergo sum.

To awake one morning
(as in the Kafka story)
to find one has become
irreversibly alien
to one's familiar world;
whom one's dearest shun.

Only the ritual slim
negotiate the narrow stairs,
fit a place to sit
at the polite table.
Je mange, donc je maigris.

I read *The Times*
with my breakfast egg,
check the sports results,
start on the Clue Across.
Cogito, ergo sum.

FEAR OF FLYING

Not so much the fear of
coming down, as of going up;
of developing that incredible
lightness of being by which
the hallowed angels fly,
in defiance of life's gravity.

Of leaving our attachment
to the ground, the earthbound
tenancies and claims that fix
us like guy-ropes firmly to
some point in present time,
anchored in the history of now.

Brave aviators are not unlike
Christian mystics or assiduous
astronomers pushing
the known human frontiers
to a Divine hinterland, while
breaking barriers of sound.

SUNRISE

Small wonder that the sun
was worshipped by the ancients;
even now, after Copernicus,
in a distracting universe,
the clutter on the skyline
(billboards, pylons, high-rise),
it is an enthralling sight.

To its early devotees,
dawnings were tremendous:
unescorted, the Sun God
entered at the eastern rim
of the pale horizon, climbing
slowly up the sky to shine
benignly on their doings.

His phased exit
in a blood-red flourish,
his due demise from time,
created a sudden vacuum
in their untrammeled lives;
a genuine sense of loss;
a cosmic sadness.

Had these people known,
or even half surmised that,
in leaving them by night,
he was visiting another clime,
in the marginality of time,
how they would have doubled
their rituals and devotions.

LIGHT

To the scientific mind,
light is the one constant
in the physical universe;
all else, including time
and space, is relative.

Significant that Egyptians,
in their ancient wisdom,
should worship the sun:
source of heat and light
it governed their plight.

As there is light of day,
there is light of understanding;
the truth *dawns* on us;
to lack knowledge
is to remain in the dark.

The Quakers and off-shoots,
the Shakers, acknowledged
an inner light guiding
the heart and mind:
a beacon for mankind.

Is not then the numinous,
in its vague awareness
of a transcendent Reality,
akin to the luminous,
the light all around?

BIOLOGIST

He tried to find the mind,
the locus of consciousness,
in the most expected places.

Dissecting monkeys' brains,
he pinpointed centers of touch,
vision, hearing and memory.

Next, he probed the cortex,
an area of grayish matter
on the cerebrum's surface.

Consciousness, he decided,
defied precise location.
Could it reside, instead,

in processes set in motion
by neurons transmitting
impulses to the brain?

David Hume had considered
that all awareness derives
from sensory perceptions.

Whereas Kant, after Descartes,
viewed it as more than
the sum of all external inputs.

Why, for example, did two people
faced with the same sunset
form different impressions?

All the while, the biologist
was using his elusive mind,
if in danger of losing it.

SONNET ON A WAKING DREAM

In this uncertain hour,
between dawn and half-light,
between desire and possession,

you wait in some ante-chamber
of recall, in that spare room
adjoining sleep, where lovers pause.

The gull's plaintive cry
gnaws at the lean edge of the day,
long at dawn's hour across
the empty borders of the bay.

Out on the deserted strand,
your feet imprint upon the sand;
your hair spills out in billows
where straying dolphins play.

ON THE BALL

Something is that loves a ball,
that has raised its game among
the key inventions of the race,
and lofted it above the field.

Football mesmerizes millions
across the globe—itself a ball—
inciting tribal rivalries,
rioting, sporadic violence.

Strikingly colorful, the pool
or snooker ball frequents
a more sedate indoor milieu,
city pub or recreation hall.

A cricket ball, though hard,
shows high finesse when sent
with varied pace and spin,
as Yorkers, Googlies, Chinamen.

Firm and small, the golf ball
embarks on long excursions
through the pristine wilderness,
holing up on tailored lawns.

There's even one to help foretell
the future, not only at the local
fairground stall: how many of us
truly wish we had a crystal ball?

264

THE END-TIME

What is the surest sign
we are entering the end-time?

Is it global warming,
with some coming super-flood;

or escalating conflicts
at key spots round the globe?

Is it over-population
stretching thin resources;

dearth of oil and water;
a nuclear explosion?

A rogue giant asteroid
orbiting towards us?

None of these: the surest sign
is that we're daily bringing

all our records up to date
for the final audit to take place.

Archaeologists are sifting
the rich soils of history;

families are completing
detailed genealogies,

microbiologists compiling
gene sequence and data-base.

Nothing must be lost,
overlooked or left behind

when we present ourselves
as *the human race*

before the thrones of Time.

COUNTRY CHURCHES

If they shut them down
as they talk of doing,
for want of manpower,
what then may happen?

Shall Evensong no more
ring across ploughed fields
to mark the ebb of day,
as in the Middle Ages?

No feet of clay the feudal
lord and his stout villeins,
converging by country lanes
to chant, indeed to pray.

What flower-strewn path
for young village lovers
to trip lighter down for
having tied the knot?

What place for a second
Betjeman to wonder round;
or another Thomas Gray to
pen his churchyard elegy?

Shall the countryside
soon fall back fallow,
in the rut of time allow
the fruitful propagation

of more primitive seeds:
nature-worship, animism,
or even darker creeds?
What then shall we reap?

SONGS OF PRAISE
(as televised from jail)

The stark, confining lines
of Strangeways Prison rise
like a bride-less wedding cake
above the urban deprivation
feeding its seasoned population.

The camera tracks inside,
along the chapel center aisle
dividing inmates from their
keepers; welfare workers
wear their handcuffed smiles.

They sing out in lusty pride,
in spotlight on their infamy.
I marvel at their youthfulness,
this early turn in life's giant
Ferris wheel abasing them.

At their discovery of God,
more than in the well-scrubbed
faces of the just, who hold
these tender charges hostage
to fettered forces in themselves.

THE ENGLISH ROAD

The winding road, it
undulates lovingly
through deep countryside,
hugging the hedgerows,
always in control
of its gradely progress.

It helps preserve
the unities of English life:
stone of country village,
manor house or spire;
customs centuries old.
Toad feels at home.

A motorway
has lesser social aims:
it unsettles population,
uproots, re-distributes;
erodes the farming fields,
flattens Toad, caps Mole.

It gets quite out of hand,
by some law of planners
that says we need eight lanes;
when investment in rail,
to take more freight,
would ease the strain.

Toad and Mole are characters in
Kenneth Graham's *The Wind in the Willows*.

GREEN SPACES

They appear randomly
in sudden gaps between neat
rows of houses, challenging
what is solid, pre-conceived,
filling it with uncut dreams

that lurk somewhere behind
the façade of our synthetic
world, dissolving it instantly
the moment they are so perceived
as to ignite a dormant seed.

We may let the green invade,
taking care to trim the lawn,
erase the flowers of the field
that shake like dandelions
with the jagged edge of weeds.

It may only advance so far,
to the edge of symmetry;
out there in the open country
there is no lawn, no geometry,
green spaces shape it all.

HOSPITAL IN DEMOLITION

The wards are half-erected now,
disinfected by the freshness of
the morning air; open to emergencies
in planning, beyond the care
of patients and their piteous welfare.

Plaster hangs like torn bandages
not yet baptized in blood:
yellow-pale, as if no longer
clean enough, nor deep enough,
to swab the cuts in public health.

The cries are lost of those
who lingered here in pain,
uncertainty and fear; alone,
because suffering is personal,
it will not stretch to other beds.

Alone in the dim ward-nights
they slipped peacefully away,
uncomplaining, often unobserved;
when morning and the day-nurse
found them, they were gone.

TOMBSTONES

They are markers on a board
(the game-board of our lives,
with no monopoly). Each street
must be vacated in its turn;
each property given up at call,
or put into a common trust
for up-and-coming players.

They rear up stark, immobile,
mute as to what path lies beyond.
They halt the ghost of progress
to a point, depending often on
a lucky throw. Chance encounters
or events can change it all, deceive
us with a sudden winning streak.

The mortgage is soon paid
on our souls; remaining debts
are written down to nought.
Markers show how far we get,
not how we fall, unless
by chance we fall in battle;
then they call out name, number, rank.

The slain are privileged players
on the board; equally its sacrificial pawns.

COSMIC NIETZSCHE
Einmal ist Keinmal

There are myriad stars
in the Milky Way;
countless other galaxies
in the observable universe;
beyond the black holes,
an explosion of realms
as yet unexplored.

As individual units
of the viable life
on the one planet,
of all heavenly bodies
known to be inhabited,
are we but specks of dust
in the cosmic eye?

Or do we have destiny?
Friedrich Nietzsche avers
that each unique instance
of human awareness
recurs to infinity.
Are we already launched
on a timeless trajectory?

ON READING TEILHARD DE CHARDIN

Love is much more than
the sentimental face we see
in romantic novels, films;
all forms of natural life
in some sense are in love.

Animals display courtship,
loyalty and parental care;
there's a basic drive
towards union evident
even when molecules pair.

These combine into higher
viable forms, the progeny
of an on-going natural love
building on itself to form
ever more complex entities.

Love breaks the surface
in human consciousness;
no longer blind, it binds us
at the deepest level of being,
saves us from chaos and despair.

A perfect world is no
Utopian dream, but the
end-result of an on-going
evolutionary process
striving towards fulfillment.

It will ultimately embrace
all men and all things:
authentic love of self,
of family and friends,
of the natural environment.

SIR ISAAC NEWTON
(1642-1727)

The great astronomer,
savant and mathematician
viewed the universe
as a vital extension
of the Divine Being,
the ultimate reality
behind appearances,
behind transient forms.

If a creator-spirit
is inherent in all things,
as inscrutable mover
behind the scenes,
He preserves the unity
of the universal drama
unfolding before us;
the ghost *in* the machine.

Is our individual role
something we discover;
or is it cast for us,
scripted but unseen?
Actors we all must be,
on or off Broadway or
the Comedia del'Arte;
no hugging the wings.

YOUNG HEADS

It's an intriguing thought
that each time we set foot
outside our own house
we are pelted by radiation
coming from Big Bang,
the birth of the universe.

Atoms building our bodies
are from the same source:
our age is not in decades,
but in billions of years;
we have been in existence
since the dawn of time.

Understanding all this,
we share the universal mind
(atoms themselves are blind);
older than the hills,
it includes racial memory,
behavioral syndromes,

dream times, archetypes.
In this immense collective
personhood is unique;
within decades it peaks,
putting young heads on
old shoulders, so to speak.

ANIMISM IN LAPLAND

Food offerings may
still today be seen
strung to uplifted branches
of silver birch trees.

Divinity was found
in nature, in the things
that heaved and stirred,
in the wind that breathed.

In parameters of daily life,
the powers that ruled
the unencumbered tundra
of an arctic world;

in cycles of birth and death,
hunting and the seasons'
slow rotation from deep
midwinter solstice

to the short-lived burst
of summer over mosses,
lichen, reindeer herds,
lynx, fox and wolverine.

TRUTH

It resembles a message
corked up in a bottle
cast adrift on the ocean;
to be read, if at all,
across final horizons.

Somewhere afloat,
it exists in a vacuum,
hermetic, inviolate,
from the critical moment
it goes overboard.

Testimony in camera,
deliberations of juries,
secrets of confessionals,
these are well-sealed
and drift on before us.

Or truth may surface
and swim for survival
in a sea of semblance,
half-truth, fudges, lies,
conflicting evidence.

UNSEENS
(Notes towards a dictionary definition)

Passages of prose or poetry
in classical Greek or Latin
feared by young examinees
for overtones of the unknown
(or unknowable). One could
even buy sets of unseens
(from prior academic years),
with the unique proviso that
they had been seen.

The mote in one's own eye;
secret longings and desires;
unedited versions of others,
limited editions of ourselves
(a psychiatrist might read);
the far side of the rainbow;
dark matter, wind, microbes;
magnetic fields, the antipodes.

The force informing all things,
seen, half-seen and unseen.

ROYALS

Are they a suaver,
up-market edition of ourselves,
sharper, better-dressed?
A sort of human optimum
we do not aspire to,
yet reserve within us,
an ideal paradigm?
In our finer moments,
we feel like a king.

Mystique holds good
for those who, revolutionary,
sent crowned heads to block
or guillotine; they remain
avid watchers of royalty
that survived to modern times.
Ousted monarchs stake
their exiled claims; the French
quickly regretted regicide.

Themselves once commoners
in the telescope of time,
they forged their way up
through the pack, founded
dynasties, blood-lines
sanctioned by Divine Right.
The media, working on
their human side, aim to
draw them back into the herd.

BRITONS

They invented the battle tank;
in World War 11, German panzers
proved much more efficient.

They pioneered locomotives;
yet Continental railways
everywhere outpace theirs.

Having invented soccer,
they strive to lift their game
to compete at world level.

This amateur approach,
a reluctance to outperform,
comes from the spirit of fair play

on the playing fields of Eton:
the underdog should always
have a good sporting chance.

There is something unlovely
about ruthless efficiency,
the obsession with winning

irrespective of cost.
Officers at the Armistice
agreed that the Wehrmacht

were honorable opponents;
by and large they adhered
to the broad rules of war,

as if it were a complex game
being staged to the death
on the playing fields of Eton.

CHURCH REDUNDANT

The vicar's manse is boarded up,
to keep the seekers out;
evenings, he no longer stares
at the antics of his flock
passing his study window
with a vague, distracted air.

Not whets his pen
penning mordant sermons
on the manners of the day,
which left his temple stranded
at a crossroads in their lives
they scarcely recognize.

They press doggedly on,
in search of greener pastures
of a more ephemeral kind.
The struggling, legless town
falls down around him;
populations shift their shrine.

NATIVITY

There came a child like us,
born of a virgin's blush;
in this beating human heart
stirs infinite compassion,
loud in the stable's hush.

Not that we might hear it
above the rustling straw,
with the night wildly crying,
the Old Law quietly dying,
beyond the stable door.

He came to dwell among us,
unique, anonymous;
using the fainter starlight,
clandestine, incarnate;
caught in the census crush.

CHRISTMAS MEDITATION

What believers claim
is truly incredible:
that an infinite being,
somewhere out there,
arranged for a maiden
to carry his child.

This son was surely
highly exceptional,
one of a half-dozen
who lived their span
at different times
in a different clan.

Not God at all,
but a gifted mentor
in Herodian Galilee;
too revolutionary,
he was led outside
a defeated man.

Or was he that person
in whom actual and ideal
are inextricably one,
no fumbling around,
no stumbling on;
apart, yet partisan?

HISTORY

History is the evidence of time
Marcus Tullius Cicero (106-43 BC)

CAMBRIAN

Early forms of marine life
set forth very gingerly on
those primeval odysseys
through the forming oceans,
half a billion years ago.

Wrapped up well in shells,
as if the concept of motion,
so original, unprecedented
in its way, was too frail
to accept uncovered risk.

These pioneering mollusks
delved into the sea bed,
or elected to explore
the marine undergrowth,
its tall fronds of sea-lilies.

Others did not venture far:
corals were content to form
well-knit living colonies;
perhaps they simply lacked
a sense of adventure.

Or did they from the outset
possess some inner vision,
a deeply-felt instinct
for the wonders of nature,
for the beauties of the reef?

HOMO ERECTUS

You left tools lying around
at Olduvai and 'Ubeidiya
over a million years ago,
before turning east and west.

Quite suddenly re-surfaced
over a million years later
on a quiet Sussex beach,
with much the same tool-kit.

Being an original eolithic
was evidently a very slow,
infinitely painstaking process,
a long fondling of flints.

It was a kind of golden age,
of small, scattered populations;
abundance of roots and berries;
mink, deer, the odd rhinoceros.

There was surely no onus
to rush headlong for the Bronze;
the simple life was too inviting,
yet too short, too idyllic.

STONE-AGE FLUTISTS
(30,000 BC)

With ingenuity enough
to pierce the wing-bones
of dead vultures,
positioning the holes
at regular intervals,
they made pure music
on their tonic flutes,
based on an eight-note
non-chromatic scale.

Squatting by
a narrow cave-mouth,
or on a promontory,
what mesmerizing effect
did their playing have
on the local wildlife?
Did it draw them,
Pan-like, slowly closer
for the kill?

Or was the main motif
to charm their wives
sitting round the cave
at night, the day's
decisive hunting done,
acoustics of the sky
augmenting all sound,
fresh venison spitting
over an open fire?

BONE CALENDAR
(*Grotte du Tai*, 10,000 BC)

They had no problem
with the concept of day,
succeeded by night
descending stealthily
to the mouths of caves.

As each day dawned,
someone recorded it,
systematically chipping
a piece of smooth bone
with sharpened stone.

A thousand sunrises
inscribed in sequence
show no mean devotion
on the calendarist's part
to chronological arts.

Perhaps he was clocking
a solitary spell, lost
or cast out by his kin;
the keeping of faith
with an hour-glass mate.

The days are arranged
in what seem to be years;
which may well indicate
beginning of knowledge
of the motions of spheres.

STONEHENGE

On ranging Salisbury Plain
stark, configured megaliths,
freezing our idea of time,
guard their mute significance.

Lost to us, they held it fast
for bands of prehistoric men
hauling them huge distances
by sea from western Wales.

This massive masonry,
of sarsen and bluestone,
stands undiminished through
the cold erosion of the centuries.

Its dramatic presence
plays now to empty stalls,
where former solstice rituals
beguiled the ancient Celts.

A monument to firm beliefs
within the breast of early man,
who looked for clear meanings
through chinks in a dark mass.

SEAFOOD CHAINS

When staple sources failed
(from migrations of game
or shortfalls of fruit),
they harvested the sea,
leaving piles of shell debris
hundreds of miles along
north Atlantic coastlines.

Uncharted oceans
and pristine beaches
freely greeted them,
before defensive walls,
groins and breakwaters
subdued the wilder sirens
of these early seas.

What led them to prize open
clam and oyster shells,
if not from watching waders
break them with their beaks
on rocks and open strands
they went down to combing
driftwood for their fires?

TOLLUND MAN

In Iron Age Jutland,
with a noose of sinew
tugging at your throat
(no other tell-tale sign
of rude strangulation;
no choking tongue),
looking as if serenely
drifted into deep sleep,
you took your cryptic
history down with you
to the inky, brackish
waters of the bog.

Of the tribe of Jutes,
an old Germanic race
path-finding its way
deep into Scandinavia,
was your untimely death
a fertility offering to
some avid local god?
Or case unproven,
like that of Lindow Man
found similarly configured
in a north of England
pool of sphagnum moss?

CITHARIST OF KAROS
(*circa* 2500 BC)

Quite lacking hands
(the arms are cut off
just above the elbow),
on his low-pitched stool
he still soulfully plucks
at his stringless cithar,
the lyric instrument
perched on one knee,
his head tilted back,
perhaps in rapture
at his own *pianissimo*;
or in salute to Euterpe.

This harmonious figure
leans into the abstract,
putting one freely in mind
of a modern sculpture,
by Henry Moore or Jean Arp,
in its simplicity of line
abdicating detail.
Enough here to convey
the *idea* of the art
of playing the cithar;
of the scope of music
in an ancient time.

PERSEPOLIS

Darius's abandoned palace
dominates the razed city,
its stepped entrances lined
with bas-reliefs of early Aryans,
Persian guards flexing muscle
across vast desert satrapies:
a world of griffin, ibex, lion;
tribute come by horse or camel.

Arts, revels, festivals are
figments of deserted halls;
cryptic rituals of kingship
focus on an open throne-room;
the intrigues taking shape
in more deceptive places
so much *souffle* blowing
through lost power vacuums.

Lust for power on power
had this ruler of the world,
Achaemenid king of kings,
tilt his long lance west
across the Hellespont;
a winged, youthful Greek,
relentless, pursued him
to the death in Bactria.

JOSEPH OF NAZARETH

Not much is ever said
about Saint Joseph;
a kind of tactful silence
has been maintained
down the spent centuries
for one whose wedded wife
was found, against all odds,
to be with child.

Joseph soldiers on,
always in the background,
somewhere in the ark
of his carpenter's shop;
with no hint of suspicion
of events that lay ahead
when he taught his son
the art of shaping wood.

The day came soon enough
when carpenters hewed
the heavy beams of wood,
to form a sort of tree
on which to raise the son;
no one records his father
at the scene, as if the years
had quietly intervened.

TRADITORS

One thinks of the early Church
in terms of a calendar of
virgins, saints and martyrs;
like the acolyte Tarcisius,
stoned to death on his way
to administer the sacrament
to a sick parishioner.

As of clandestine groups
leaving scratched greetings
in the Roman soil; meeting
in the haven of safe houses,
wind-stirred upper rooms,
labyrinthine catacombs,
for insecure communions.

Like any underground,
they had their weaker links;
who, to insure against arrest,
surrendered scriptural texts
to thought police, betrayed
the symbols of the faith,
the cryptic clues to rendezvous.

MYRRH

As one of three precious gifts
offered by trekking magi
at the Infant's lowly crib,
it would be readily accepted.

Bled in tears of resin
from a weeping incense tree,
it was prized by the ancients
for perfumes and cosmetics.

Medicinal applications
(as antiseptic, astringent,
healing balm) were indicated
well into the Middle Ages.

At the hour of crucifixion,
Roman soldiers, not unkind,
offered it to their victims
mixed liberally with wine.

A final act of humanity
by hardened executioners
to deliver a heavy sedative;
Jesus, records Mark, refused it.

Some claim that He survived,
revived by bitter aloes;
in that counter-event, myrrh
too may have been present.

NAVIGATION

Sturdy commercial barges
to navigate the Rhine
were floated by the Romans
for transporting the yield
of northern vineyards
to bibbers farther south;
a good Mosel even then
had bouquet *and* cachet.

They dug deep harbors
on navigable rivers
to facilitate trade between
the far-flung parts of
an expanding empire;
goods by ship went faster
than those sent overland,
by caravan to Samarkand.

Large trading vessels
stood off from the shore;
squads of smaller craft
served as local ferries,
loading the waiting hulls
with stone amphorae
holding olive oil or wine;
sacks of grain, cured hams.

CONSTANTINE THE GREAT
(285-337)

Proclaimed emperor
by the garrison at York
on the death of his father,

his first edict banned
persecution of Christians
begun under Diocletian.

Battling towards Rome,
he saw a cross in the sky:
By this sign conquer!

He took little time
reuniting the empire,
establishing Christianity

as the official religion;
but was pragmatic enough
to tolerate pagans.

As head of the Church,
he quickly inaugurated
a new, muscular orthodoxy;

his council at Nicaea
got the bishops to agree
on a universal creed.

He postponed baptism
until much later in life,
so that the crimes

and moral compromises
of a prolonged power-play
would be washed away.

CAPPADOCIANS

On conversion by St. Paul,
who wrote them letters,
they lived in relative calm
for successive centuries
under a broad Pax Romana,
in a quasi-lunar landscape
formed by layer on layer
of dense volcanic ash.

At some point their king,
prompted by his seers,
aimed to relocate
his people underground,
where they literally carved
labyrinthine townships
extending several miles
into the soft, malleable rock.

They foresaw the danger
of marauding warlords
coming a long way off;
perhaps years away
in the slow march of time,
to lay elaborate plans
to vanish, as it were,
from the face of Asia Minor.

Carefully-placed shafts
maintained oxygen levels,
fresh water came from wells;
consecrated chapels stored
fine communion wines;
dark, secret passages led
every which way, some
of them still sealed today.

THE WHITHORN DIG

They are scraping slowly down
through the sedimentary record
for a hint of Saint Ninian,
apostle of the Southern Picts,
on a mission rigged in Rome.

Disclosing layer upon layer
of early Christian history:
how short-lived bones were laid
in shallow, cycled graves;
how Galloway was saved.

When the *hwiterne* was built;
the priory church and shrine
inviting pilgrimage and trade,
its litany of kings and queens
to Mary Stuart's reign.

The wary, woaded Picts
retreated deep into the loch
at the haste of Latin strangers;
to preach to a sea of heads
demanded depths of faith.

Hwiterne is the Anglo-Saxon name of present-day
Whithorn on
      The Solway Firth; it means: At the White House.

CEMENTARIUS MAGISTER OPERIS
Ars longa, vita brevis (1)

A master stonemason
of the later Middle Ages,
he oversaw the construction
of our Gothic cathedrals.

Not content with cement,
he would often incorporate
conceptual innovations
of design and ornament.

The sum-total of these,
introduced over time,
helped create and establish
our true national style.

He made running repairs
following partial collapse,
reaching those parts
former masons had skimped.

Technology was not given,
it was slowly acquired,
to raise the great spires
over burgeoning shires.

It would not be unknown
for an artisan to devote
his entire working life
to a unique building site;

nor for a given minster
to engross the careers
of successive generations
of worshipful stonemasons.

(1) Art is long, life is short

ST. WILFRID'S, RIBCHESTER
(*circa* 650 AD)

What did Drogo,
the first-recorded pastor,
then survey, before
the French incumbents
learned their Latin names?

Lean meadows, Ribble-drained,
the crow still haunts in
swooping search of prey;
the Roman fort that held
hostile Brigantes at bay.

He lifted Roman stone to
build his church, bequeathed
its stark antiquity of nave;
buried his dead in simple graves,
his churchyard moated by

the Ribble's seaward sway.
He preached before Wycliffe's
Lollards raised rebel chants
and anglicized their prayers;
but was not in time to read

The Canterbury Tales.
The Black Death had not yet
passed his way; but the crows
circle still as they did then,
over Druid bones and Christian.

WULFRIC

Man is born free; everywhere he is in chains.
Jean-Jacques Rousseau

He was a villein
(from the Latin *villanus),*
owned by his feudal lord,
whose fields he tilled
so many days a week;
whom he brought fresh eggs
at Eastertide, a custom
that survives chocolatized.
In return he had the use
of a few strips of land
to provide for himself
and his several dependents.

Even granted the freedom
that he daily craved,
his routine would not
have altered in the least.
He would continue tilling
those very same fields,
with this material difference:
his deepest feelings about
himself; awareness that
his service was by willing
giving; that he would live
and die a free man.

Villanus is Latin for villager

WINDMILLS

Visible for many roods,
they loomed large
in medieval landscapes;
as in the imagination,
for Don Quixote to tilt
at one on Rosinante.

A monk's weather eye
had seen the potential
of harnessing the elements,
risking the ribaldry of
professional skeptics
as the sails were raised.

The novel technology
soon sold its charms:
one wooden structure
served the milling needs
of manorial estates
and small scattered farms.

The Luttrell Psalter
gives a fine illustration
of a mill in working trim;
something to sing about,
perhaps in plainchant,
when the wind blew thin.

VENERABLE BEDE
(c.672-735)

To him we are indebted
for much of our knowledge
of Angle-Saxon England,
as for firmer foundations
in historical method.

Lacking written records,
sifting of hard facts became
an occupational hazard
for conscientious chroniclers;
there were too many hacks.

It was an age of credulity,
when society as a whole
laid great emphasis on faith;
omens, miracles and signs
wowed the popular mind.

A cloister chronologist,
Bede dated later events
from the coming of Christ,
introducing general use
of the tag Anno Domini.

He spent time at Lindisfarne
on contemporary polemics,
fixing movable feasts;
that might seem academic
to the post-modern mind.

KING JOHN (1167-1216)

Vigorously extending
Henry 1l's system
of dispatching agents
to administer justice
throughout the realm,
he advanced Common Law.

Court sessions were open,
with evidence presented
and witnesses called;
no secret denunciations
to faceless inquisitors
(the custom in Europe),

torture, confession by duress.
This royal justice,
was eagerly sought
by subjects confident
of its even-handedness
alike to rich and poor.

Ironic in a way
that up-in-arms barons,
after ruinous campaigns,
bound the sovereign himself,
by a written charter,
within his own domains.

Magna Carta became
a seminal instrument
in political history,
beginning the process
by which modern states
acknowledge the Rule of Law.

A ROYAL PREROGATIVE

Some early English kings
expired from over-indulging
their right royal appetites;
the occasion might be
a surfeit of lampreys,
undigested watermelons,
over-ripe peaches.

How were such exotic fruits
procured for the tables
of this cool sceptred isle,
before the growth of foreign
trade? The royal domains,
at Henry 11's marriage,
included balmy Aquitaine.

Kings could pick peaches,
as it were, in their own backyard,
until allegiances changed
and the French monarchy,
aided by Joan of Arc,
asserted dynastic claims
to Anjou, Gascony and Maine.

MEDIEVAL PARLIAMENTS

It was Simon de Montfort
who thought of including
knights from the shires
and freemen from towns,
to offset the heavy presence
of barons and clerics
when policy was formed,
justice meted, monies raised.

Anticipating perils,
these hardy commoners
set forth on days-long
treks to the royal court,
by lawless highways,
flooding fords, giving bridges;
beset by outlaws, conmen,
beggars, pardoners, rogues.

Descent of many delegates
on one place put a strain
on available accommodation.
Squabbles and spats arose;
chaos and crime were part
of the fabric of court life;
friendships were cemented,
and a man might find a wife.

LITTLE JOHN

He has lain undisturbed
in Hathersage churchyard
these many centuries
since his best adventures
with young Robin Hood;
both were outlawed on
the defeat of their leader,
Simon de Montfort.

The earl had revolted
against the fiscal imposts
of Henry the Third,
an absentee tax-gatherer
who exported these tolls
to European foundations,
ruling England from Rome
or Paris, rarely from home.

John's powerful bow,
drawn by this giant of a man
at the Battle of Evesham,
once framed the church nave;
less bellicose echoes
can be raised over ale
at *The Scotsman's Pack*
downhill from the grave.

CONVERSOS

Sephardic Jews
transferred in droves
to the medieval church,
to escape deportation
from Ferdinand's Spain.

Under constant watch
for counter-indications
to genuine faith,
they were often denounced
and 'tested' for heresy.

Not even as converts
could they count themselves
safe from discrimination,
such was the weight
of the vertical state.

At length across Europe
a strong reaction set in:
long Wars of Religion
brought in their wake
the concept of tolerance.

This could only mean
true freedom of belief;
yet even in our day
prisoners of conscience
remain behind bars.

ACOMA, NEW MEXICO

Towering skyscrapers
were hundreds of years
into a metropolitan future.

Perched high on a mesa,
in sight of the Rio Grande,
rose this city of the sky.

Blocks of terraced dwellings
stood one atop another,
in Pueblo Indian style.

Each level was divided
into communicating rooms
for housing family groups.

It was a keen experience,
a sort of early prototype
of high-rise apartment life.

Healthy too, with fresh air,
unadulterated produce
and lots of ladder-work.

But it was also a Masada
for much of its community,
who leapt from the walls

down several hundred feet
of sheer cliff-face,
to escape Conquistadors.

AZTEC GARDENS

When the morning sun
rose above the Andes,
it shone benignly on
gardens of the Aztecs:
artificial islands,
rectangular in shape,
kissing, drifting
at the edge of lakes.

Lacustrine acres,
they were set aside,
like allotment plots,
to cater for the ebb
and flow of population,
cycles of drought and flood
being swiftly eliminated
by on-site irrigation.

Hanging gardens
were seen at Babylon
and marveled at;
steep terraces hewn
into island hillsides
maximized the yield
in yams beloved
of early Polynesians.

Floating gardens
one could wade out to,
tend with leaking can
or nimbly swim around,
an hibiscus gripped
betweens one's teeth,
surely this had been
gardening's *dernier cri*.

JOHN WYCLIF (1328-84)

Born a Yorkshireman,
he set an uncompromising face
against abuses of the time
the pope escaped to Avignon.
Dividing Christendom.

He presaged the Reformation,
defining the abiding church
less as formal institution,
more as mystical communion
of all the truly faithful.

Seeking a purer strain,
he denounced the traffic
in indulgences, clergy fallings,
the sale of church livings,
exploitation of the poor.

He cause the Bible to be read
in English by itinerant bands
clad in simple russet smocks
and bearing staves to lend
more emphasis to the Word.

His trenchant sermons
bit deep into society's soft core;
his treatise championed the king
against arrears of papal dues
claimed off John Lackland's heirs.

ROBERT CAMPIN:
Portrait of Robert de Masmines (d.1430)

A sturdy, stocky man,
his stock-in-trade was
fealty to his feudal overlord;
chevalier sans peur et
sans reproche, he fell
at the razing of Bouvignes.

Like a siege-tower himself
assailed, he sailed
into the thick of battle;
a flailing war machine
arming to the teeth
in awesome panoply.

Arrow, sword or lance,
by whatever means he fell,
his end was monumental
to the faithful retinue
who bore him sorely down,
dismantled him, trekked him
in sections from the field.

His life had been assembled
for dismemberment in battle;
valor was its virtue,
death its fighting chance.

LE CIMETIERE DES INNOCENTS
(*circa* 1450)

In fifteenth-century Paris,
it was a popular place to meet:
society came there to parade
the latest fashions, exchange
the day's light gossip strolling
in the dust to dust and heat.

La guerre des cent ans
made them familiars of death,
its clinical detail exploited
by the Church's fecund preachers;
by graphic artists of the day
portraying its anatomy.

Children innocently played,
kicked a vacant skull around
or hid among the open graves;
harlots resurrected trade
in tenser, less recoiling flesh
within the pale of hermits' cells.

They shut themselves away
from this unreconciling world,
to pamper their ascetic lives
beside man's frail mortality;
deaf to the *danses macabres*
raging everywhere outside.

TITIAN

The late-Venetian artist
used his wife as a model
to portray popular figures
in religious paintings.

This might be to invest her
with the subject's own graces,
the way men idealize women,
(if they do not also idolize).

This practice helped liberate
the representation of saints,
which by the Middle Ages
had become static and stylized.

One effect was to perpetuate
the signora's youthful beauty,
beatifying her humanity,
while humanizing sanctity.

Enter Hans Holbein:
men too were canvassed,
through court portraiture,
for a framed immortality.

ERASMUS
(1466-1536)

A native of Rotterdam,
second son of a priest,
he was a firm advocate
of conventional wedlock
for the regular clergy.

Condemning endemic wars,
whether of pope or prince,
this shrewd theologian
urged men to revisit
the true gospel spirit.

A subtle precursor
of the northern reformers,
he stood for the renewal
of church and society
by learning and piety.

Considered to be the first
true European liberal,
he chose the middle road
between reform and tradition,
as averting deep schism.

The divisive issues
of the Reformation era,
to this key humanist were
mere matters of emphasis,
not of hardened opinion.

LEO X (*Giovanni de Medici*)
(1475-1521)

Singing along with the violins,
this high-Renaissance pope
enlivened the solemn confines
of the Vatican escorted by
his court musicians.

Such tuneful progress
led him past Greek statues
in the Belvedere to his own
frescoed chapel, to extol
the work of Michelangelo.

Investing the Eternal City
with vast artistic wealth,
he impoverished it spiritually
with indulgences tapping
the faithful's credibility.

Out stag-hunting, it is said,
when they brought him the Bull
to muzzle Martin Luther;
he signed it absent-mindedly,
keeping one eye on his quarry.

BATTLE OF TOWTON
(Wars of the Roses, 1461)

In the manicured grounds
of an old Tudor mansion,
they serve afternoon tea
with strawberries and cream.

In extending the gardens,
excavations unearthed
the site of this battlefield
and a mass burial ground.

Contemporary records
show no quarter was given,
a verdict confirmed by
new forensic research.

On quitting the field,
Lancastrians were trapped,
cut down, dismembered,
crudely dispatched.

Devoid of the vaunted
medieval code of chivalry,
this was a mere power-play
to advance regal claims.

The genteel conventions
of civilized living,
are built upon conflict,
mayhem and killing.

DEATH OF RICHARD 111 (1485)

What an arresting sight
it must then have been
to observe an English king,
an able, seasoned warrior
bearing the royal coat-of-arms,
charge full-tilt downhill
with his household knights
in awesome battle panoply,
to take out his adversary,
the young Henry Tudor,
on Bosworth Field.

Tudor's bodyguard of foot,
swordsmen and pikemen
backing him from Wales,
closed ranks around him
and stood their ground;
the last Yorkist monarch,
named Richard Crookback,
a readily identifiable,
high-value, marked target,
was repulsed, unhorsed,
beleaguered, slain.

WILLIAM TYNDALE
(1492-1536)

It fell to John Skelton,
Henry V111's poet laureate,
to pen diatribes in rhyme
against English translators
and printers of bibles.

The Establishment was bent
on the retention of Latin,
which reformers considered
locked the gospels away
from the ken of the faithful.

Bringing the Scriptures
directly to the public
in handy pocket editions,
was one way of activating
a more personalized faith,

which would depend less
on clerical mediation
or mechanical formulae,
and help foster the growth
of individual conscience.

His unstinting labors
gave a strong new impetus
to the use of English as
standard literary medium,
come the age of Elizabeth.

MARGARET CRANMER

Like Duerer, Melanchthon,
she hailed from Nuremberg,
which had opted Protestant;
the king's chaplain was there
on a clandestine mission
to vet Luther's position.

When her husband was plunged
into the Canterbury See
(to pilot Henry's divorce),
she remained out of sight,
behind the wainscoting,
as it were; a closet wife.

What subtle influence
did this first helpmeet have
on the future confection
of the established church,
after several centuries
of canonical celibacy?

She introduced, no doubt,
a hint of domesticity
into fusty church affairs;
comforts of the family manse,
and the now well-outed role
of English vicar's wife.

ELIZABETHAN LIFE

They spent as much on sauces
as on the rich meat dishes,
of which a good half-dozen
comprised a merchant's dinner;

drank copiously from cups
French and Canary wines,
quaffed ale German-style,
puffed at the novel pipe.

The doublets young men wore
had a soft velvet sheen,
sleeves slashed with silk,
blue or goose-turd green.

So clad they would stroll
down to the Southwark Globe;
take in some bear-baiting,
follow the cock-fight code.

Thousands were impoverished
by enclosures of the common;
forgotten, they trod highways
as beggars, conmen, rogues.

EDMUND CAMPION
(1540-1581)

A veritable champion
of the old Catholic faith,
he was trained by Jesuits
to spearhead a mission
to return England to the fold;
martyrdom was in prospect
before he ever set foot
on his dauntless road.

When Gregory X111
re-charged the papal Bull
'deposing' the English queen,
releasing her subjects from
allegiance to the throne,
Campion went underground,
meeting in great secrecy,
hiding in priest-holes.

With England living daily
under threat of invasion,
promoting the old devotions
all too readily assumed
treasonable overtones.
Campion's final verdict
on mounting the scaffold:
we traveled for souls.

ELIZABETH 1 AND MARY STUART

Elizabeth Tudor,
at considerable risk
to her personal safety,
showed great reluctance
to move against Mary,
who plotted against her.

Seared on her mind
from a tender age
were the exacted lives
of her father's wives,
serially cut short
as she romped at court.

Ravens crowded the Tower
those innocent years
of her motherless youth;
small wonder she shrank,
in astute maturity,
from final solutions.

She looked forward
towards an enlightened age
of religious tolerance
and freedom of conscience,
not wishing to open
'a window on men's souls'.

IVAN 1V VASILYEVICH
(1530-1584)

For all his many crimes,
there was a quixotic side
to this measureless man
(soubriquet *the Terrible*),
who offered to resign
to pursue a quieter life
in the English countryside.

Perhaps he'd had enough
of tortuous boyars' plots;
of repulsing the Tatars
from Muscovy's frontiers;
of dynastic concerns
not dissimilar to those
of our Tudor thrones.

For incarnadine acts
he felt fully justified
by dint of Divine Right;
whatever the event,
in a crimson century
overshadowed by fate,
there were reasons of state.

A hint of romance, too,
in his mooting a match
with a lady-in-waiting
at Queen Elizabeth's court,
having heard good reports
of our tenor of life,
of the true English rose.

COURTESANS

They attained high status
in sixteenth-century Venice
by preserving the virtue
of girls and married women.

Decked in jewels and finery,
the top end of the trade,
in private luxury-suites,
led privileged lives.

Not quite kept mistresses,
more like refined geishas,
they entertained with music
and informed conversation.

The profession's lower end
eluded watchful vice patrols
and guardians of the city
by cross-dressing as men.

Fully availing themselves
of the earnings potential
of slipping in and among
long canal-side shadows,

they plied their ancient trade
with the tacit compliance
of the wily, worldly-wise,
amenable gondoliers.

PIETER BRUEGHEL: *Return of the Hunters*

This picture tells us more than
many histories. A mere handful
appear to be working outside
the village inn with a broken sign
no one has bothered to repair;
a little slipshod this, suggesting
just a touch of *laissez faire.*

The rest—I estimate a round
four dozen—disport themselves
on the frozen surface of the lakes:
one reserved for curling; skating,
sledging on the other, with groups
of chill spectators standing by.
Much like youngsters they all were,
in that land of innocents before
the birth-pangs of industrial man.

We gauge the distance roughly
between the settlements lying
scattered under snow-wrapped eaves,
within the peal of parish bells;
and estimate a journey time
for the rush-cart man heading
down towards the middle distance
along a silent avenue of trees.

Upon this scene the homeward
hunters come, stealing it with
a powerful foreground presence.
Their footfalls have a firmness
of intent amid the universal play;
from fruitless toil heads are bent,
in silence of exhaustion or defeat.

Followed by a pack of skulking dogs
that nose the grudging earth
for scents they might have lost;
watched aloft by four sardonic rooks
immobile on the leafless boughs.

GALILEO GALILEI

From atop the high tower
he demonstrated the speed
of free-falling cannon balls
for the worthies of Pisa.

Such empirical methods
soon began to unravel
the threads of Aristotle's
scientific apparel.

He mounted a challenge
to the medieval outlook,
which leaned heavily
(like some tower of the mind)

towards geo-centricity,
the established belief
in a motionless earth
as hub of the universe.

The Copernican view,
that earth orbits the sun,
proved the ultimate snub
to a prevailing orthodoxy

bent on linking theology
to classical knowledge;
to quarrel with Aristotle
contradicted the Scriptures.

Imprisoned and hauled
before Roman Inquisitors,
he was forced to retract
his considered opinions,

to desist from teaching
and learned discussions,
under permanent house arrest
in his native Florence.

THOUGHTS ON TRINITY SUNDAY

Surveyors retained
at the court of the Sun King
mapped France in triangles;
they gave each location,
as viewed from a steeple
or the summit of a hill,
its due correlations.

Not entirely at sea,
the early navigators,
dusting their astrolabes,
discovered a rondure
to replace the flat earth,
once they had fathomed
the parallax of stars.

As we may discern
the same basic shapes
in our everyday universe:
how a child relates to
its parents; magic circles,
the eternal triangle;
Round Table, trio *con brio*.

ROB ROY MacGREGOR

He began his long career
in conventional fashion,
as a reputable trader
in black Highland cattle.

A market recession
found him unable to repay
the credit advanced him
by chiefs of large clans.

They seized his home
and estates at Inversnaid,
his ancestral abode on
the shores of Loch Lomond.

Partly out of revenge,
as much as from need,
he extorted a living
from rich cattle breeders,

marauding the braes
with his kilted companions,
stealing from lairds
to provide for the poor.

When pursued by the law,
he fled to the Duke of Argyle's
wild, extensive domains,
dying in bed, of old age.

BENJAMIN FRANKLIN
(1706-1790)

A self-made man,
versatile and practical,
he embodied Quaker doctrine
of a guiding inner light.

You might find him printing
the *Philadelphia Gazette*;
or composing maxims
for his popular almanac.

A friend of Wedgwood
and of inventor James Watt,
his research into electricity
was honored at Oxford.

To him we owe lightning rods,
a prototype fire brigade,
people's militias (to fend off
the French and Native Americans).

His stand against slavery,
as against vested interests,
propelled him to prominence
in national politics.

A life-enhancing Puritan
short on formal education,
he was a sort of homespun,
frontier Renaissance man.

ADLER VERSUS FREUD

In treating neuroses,
Freud viewed the libido
as the fundamental drive
of human nature;
but he did not analyze
the merchandising
of this key insight
into how we function:
sex works wonders.

Alfred Adler,
Freud's contemporary,
saw our main motivation
in power over others:
the possessive lover,
gulag commandant,
Hitler, Napoleon,
corporate raider,
sadist, blackmailer.

In scheme or intrigue
at throne or boardroom,
campaign headquarters,
sex (as of a Mata Hari)
is an elegant weapon;
deadly, but secondary
to broader objectives.
The true orgies are
the power games played.

PETER BAUM
(World War 1 poet, d. 1916)

A gentle Rhinelander
with a schoolmasterly air,
he served as stretcher-bearer
on the Western Front.

He evokes a rainbow,
its promise of an early peace
after the lightning storm;
the hope was still-born.

Doves, harbingers,
flee into the setting sun,
their gentler omens gone.
Looms instead the nightmare

of exploding shells,
the splintering of limbs,
the lowering of the mind's
threshold of endurance.

The lull does not embrace him
digging graves in the cool
of evening for the day's dead:
shrapnel arrows head.

RAINER MARIA RILKE
(1875-1926)

He is renting a farm
on the north-German plain,
attempting domesticity
with painter-wife Clara.

He transfers to Paris,
as secretary to Rodin,
who points him to the zoo
for observation practice.

Often on night trains
between European cities,
he is invariably met
at these near-destinations;

perchance by Benvenuta,
a young concert pianist
who is drawn *obligato*
to his lyrical spirit.

He mixes with titles,
guests with a princess
on the Adriatic skyline;
wrestles with angels.

Lionized in Berlin
in the nineteen-twenties,
the now celebrated poet
disclaims sudden fame

to lead a hermit's life
at Chateau de Muzot,
completing the elegies
he began at Duino.

GEISHAS

Born into poor families
hard put to support them,
they were taken and trained
from a very tender age
to high degrees of etiquette
and cultural attainment.

To merit their company
and refined conversation,
warlike, itinerant samurai
devoted many months
to careful personal grooming
and fashionable attire.

These elegant women
yet wore an air of sadness,
an impenetrable pathos;
they had the beauty and style
of a most desirable bride,
yet romance was denied.

Love could never be part
of the rapport they made
with ardent male suitors
pledging lasting fidelity;
they died unsung, their remains
consigned to unmarked graves.

THE GHOST DANCE (1890)

At Geronimo's surrender,
Native-American peoples,
after conflicts with militias
spanning three centuries,
had joined reservations.

In end-game desperation,
their spirit largely broken,
a rumor rose among them
that they might turn back time
by ritual chants and mime.

Performed in 'ghost shirts',
this trance-like dance
was meant to reinstate
the world as it had been
before arrival of the whites.

Settlements, railroads, forts
would mysteriously disappear;
warrior chiefs like Tecumseh
would return to lead again,
and bison roam the plains.

Convinced that the sacred shirts
gave immunity from bullets,
a group of Sioux broke out
in a last desperate stand;
they died at Wounded Knee.

COTTON MILLS IN THE DEPRESSION
(*Oldham, Lancashire*)

They loomed up in the night,
haunted eyes wide open
with a yellow, manic light;
while the town slept on
fears of unemployment,
hunger, and of rent arrears.

At dawn they awoke cold;
their strange place-names,
read against familiar skies,
alienated homely streets
with vistas leading down
to *Cairo, Durban* and the *Nile*.

For all their awkward size,
the sheer ungainly scale
of red-brick building blocks,
they were adroitly turned
by strong resourceful boys
into forbidden toys.

They raided cobbled yards
for cast-off wicker skips
to burn on Bonfire Night;
scaled the high lodge walls
for lesser crested newts
and frogs with hooded eyes.

NEVILLE CHAMBERLAIN

Appeasement, long considered
a dirty word, branded him
as a type of moral coward.
But is this really fair?

He was a peace-loving man
from a peaceable nation
that suffered huge losses
at Ypres and the Somme.

He sought to avoid war
from his valid insight
that Stalin would profit from
a new European conflict.

Germany, by annexing Austria
and the Sudetenland, in theory
formed a formidable block
to the march of Communism.

Would Hitler rest at that?
Had Neville read *Mein Kampf*
and its expansionist program,
he might have avoided the trap.

Perhaps his Achilles heel
was his sheer inability
to get inside the mind
of so unpredictable a man.

SONDERZUEGE

They were special trains,
concealed within the railway
network's daily traffic load.

In the normality of war,
with many extra trains
specially commissioned

for the carriage of troops,
relief supplies and guns,
the *Sonderzuege* evoked
the wonder of no one.

They would be booked,
like other special trains,
through the same *Reiseburo*

that would arrange,
in less defensive times,
an enterprising holiday.

In the abnormality of war,
in the near-breakdown
of usual relationships,

in the reign of chaos,
these secret shuttle trains
with their human payload,

would run consistently,
with a smooth efficiency,
along the local railroad.

PALE MOTHER
(Berlin, 1945)

A ghost, she rises from the plain,
her face emaciated with the pain
inflicted in the loss of many sons;
the milk drained from her breasts
yields no useful nourishment.

The cold-set eastern plain
is littered with the hard remains
of war: the spiking bayonets,
the rusting shards of arms,
the barbed wire cruelly cut.

Her bloodless eyes peer out
across the cold awakening dawn,
through the hanging gables,
the vacant, splayed embrasures
where windows echo stars.

No sudden infant's gaze
alights wide-eyed upon the world;
none will rush to clasp the hem
of tattered clothes she wore
dyed in scarlet, dipped in blood.

So much she clearly understood:
the ones she early nurtured
in their fading dreams of glory,
they marched first up to the front;
the bravest and the best were lost.

HITLER'S ARCHITECT

He dwelt on the upper floors
of his own fecund mind,
in visionary future cities
designed to survive;
but claimed not to notice
less utopian programs
taking shape on the ground.

His plea at Nuremberg,
of partial complicity
in the aims of the regime,
was accepted by judges;
deemed relatively humane
in his use of slave labor,
he escaped execution.

Speer's must have been
by far the most enviable
of the manifold tasks
that fell to the servants of
the Reich: planning and design
of the way it would look
in a thousand years' time.

CHILD-SURVIVOR OF THE CAMPS

In the face of freedom
I stand and look back on
the void that enclosed me;
the frail, vagrant shapes
that might have been kin
(I struggle to remember);
mother's fleeting face;
dry bread, wet skin.

I look forward to
the fact of my survival;
the chance to unravel
coiled emotions out of
no thread; meeting someone
who might lead me blind
through the mind's vortex
towards a surer self.

I do not know it yet
(this in itself is a mercy),
but these slow searching steps
back towards personhood,
all growth in understanding
lead unerringly to this:
increased awareness of
the violence done to me.

348

POLITICAL STATUS LIMBO

What cruelty of fate,
to live in those limbos
created by regimes
themselves now defunct.

To be an official mistake
that cannot be rectified
in chronicle or book;
whom records overlook.

To inhabit a time-warp
which vanishes the past,
eliminates the future,
disorients the present.

To be a grieving to kin,
yet no true bereavement;
there being no closure,
as of grave or epitaph.

And to those dear ones
who most eagerly cling
to the flimsiest finger,
a vacuum of hope and love.

COLLAPSE OF A TOTALITARIAN STATE

In the capital's dry heart
life goes searching on,
haphazard; traffic stalls;
soldiers pause at corner cafes,
scant oases under trees.

At worst it will retreat
under the pall of night
to a defined seamy side:
unlit areas of dim streets,
doorways issuing vice.

In tunnels beneath the city,
nothing is left to chance;
each move is programmed
in advance, to subvert
the fragile innocence above.

Drawing it to secret depths
in a kind of anti-life
un-spied on by the public;
until the walls' collapse
reveals these meaner arteries.

EXILES' RETURN TO LATVIA

When Stalin marched in,
Balts were herded out
as traitors to the homeland;
banished to the gulags,
to end their lives as slaves.

Their bones were later dug
from shallow arctic graves
and shipped back home
in zipped black body-bags,
each clasping a name.

Kin gathered to receive them
in the dimmed airport lounge,
lifting their scant remains,
in augmenting silence,
as luggage off conveyors.

Across time's white tundra,
they have come full circle,
these unwilling exiles;
beginning and end is saved,
the middle un-reclaimed.

JODRELL BANK

At the terrestrial end
of a radio telescope,
they tune in to the stars,
the way we earthlings
choose classical wavelengths
and listen raptly to . . .
Eine Kleine Nachtmusik,
in preference to
Musick of the Spheres,
those orbital motions
Isaac Newton described,
by which heavenly bodies
intuitively harmonize.

The giant apparatus,
among the world's largest,
was duly inaugurated
under Astronomer Royal,
Sir Bernard Lovell,
in the county of Chester;
in good time to track
the first Russian sputnik:
the prospect this gave of
peaceful feelers in space;
or its awesome converse,
the jarring cacophony
of some future Star Wars.

COMPUTER GENESIS

Mathematical gadgets
like Charles Babbage's
Difference Engine
were likely inspired
by Adam Smith's writings
on the division of labor
in manufacturing plants.

Cogs in a machine
replaced human beings;
by isolating each task,
the device combined
arithmetical functions
(addition and subtraction)
relieving the mind.

Later inventors made
only minor adjustments;
the main impetus came
with the compelling need
for mathematical accuracy
in the engineering feats
of industrialized Europe.

If Jacquard pioneered
the use of punched cards
to program his looms
to weave textile designs,
the first true computer
was built to unravel
Nazi *Enigma* codes.

PUBLIC STATUES

Set in stone or bronze,
they occupy the space
carved out for them
in city squares, parks
and public gardens.

They occupy a place
in our consciousness,
the collective mind
that declares itself
of a piece, *en masse*,

as against injustice,
barriers of race or class;
for explorers, savants,
statesmen, pioneers
and philanthropists.

Dismantling a statue
is one seismic act:
echoes of Ozymandias,
more latterly of Lenin,
ripe for a felling.

It marks a signal break
with our conceptual past,
clearing the pedestal
of jargon and guano
for the next ideograph.

GREEN ISSUES

We once hid in tall grasses
growing wild and free,
to pick off passing game;
learned to recycle fur,
prepare a steak tartare.

Slowly we transformed the world
into a market garden,
curbing its chaotic will
into a tame estate
governed by the seasons.

Dividing it in lots
appeased our metric reason,
the hectares lovingly paced out
to yield each willing serf
his due feudal share.

Instinct leads us back
into the wild, to national parks,
the virgin countryside,
backyard barbecues,
déjeuners sur l'herbe.

As if our culinary skills
had somehow failed to cater
for our jaded appetite,
we go instead in urgent search
of wilder weeds and herbs.

SHIP TO HOTEL

The Cold War has thawed;
a redundant battleship
from a Great Power fleet
heads for its last defeat.

Unceremoniously beached
on a remote Indian coast,
it is inched daily higher
on the winch of the tide.

Thin villagers descend
on this jettisoned bounty
rolling towards them,
a rogue Spanish galleon.

They slowly dismantle it,
working out from inside,
and reduce the vast hull
into strips for the mill.

More interesting bits
(instruments, anchor, trim)
are shipped on to auctions
for chandlers to bid.

Next time you look out
from your high-rise hotel
(perhaps sighting ships),
remember its sea-going ribs.

NIMBYISM

Have we reached a stage
where we have knowledge
that is burdensome,
that we might disclaim?

Who wants nuclear bombs,
or even nuclear waste,
biological weapons,
a cloned human race?

Thousands try to stall
hazardous transportations;
cities declare themselves
nuclear-free zones.

Arriving from early times,
when a handy flint knife
was a major breakthrough
in user technology,

we survived famines, wars,
the Dark Ages, learning
abandoned or destroyed,
other burnings of books,

smallpox, bubonic plague.
Are we now so advanced
that we must unlearn
in order to survive?

CAIN ENABLED

When man chipped flints,
they were quickly adapted
as lethal arrow-heads.

The wheel was invented
and soon fixed to chariots
to harry the infantry.

After the Wright Brothers
manned the first flight,
air forces arrived.

Pasteur discovered microbes;
it wasn't too long ere
we suffered germ warfare.

Following Sigmund Freud,
it was not a big step
to psychological weapons.

When the atom was split,
bombs were produced
using nuclear fission.

In an age of cyberspace,
the internet is useful
for pursuing terrorism.

Now that we have cloning,
what combative use
shall we find for doubles?

APPENDIX

Appreciative acknowledgement is made to the following persons and institutions, who have cordially subscribed to this 70th Birthday edition:-

Paul Amatt	Saddleworth, Yorkshire, UK
John and Nancy Boschetti	Franklin, New Hampshire
Tim and Noreen Connors	Laconia, New Hampshire
Leslie and Annette Cooper	Hazel Grove, Cheshire, UK
De La Salle Brothers, GB	Oxford, England
Robert Diley	Rochester, New Hampshire
Chad Graves	Laconia, New Hampshire
Cedric Hayes	Sale, Cheshire, England
Dave and Carol Jaworski	Bury, Lancashire, England
Peter and Jane Karagianis	Gilford, New Hampshire
Judy Lund	Saddleworth, Yorkshire, UK
Elizabeth Luttrell	Bethesda, Maryland
Diane Lynch	Laconia, New Hampshire
Peter H. Mallinson	Saddleworth, Yorkshire, UK
Catharine T. Mallinson	Laconia, New Hampshire
Adrienne Mallinson	Rochester, New Hampshire
Clare M. Mallinson	Laconia, New Hampshire
John J. Mallinson	Rochester, New Hampshire
Robert and Harriet Meade	Laconia, New Hampshire
Clifton and Arlene Newell	Laconia, New Hampshire
The Pearson Family	Laconia, New Hampshire
Add Penfield	Greenwood, South Carolina
Leslie and Dora Perkins	Wolverhampton, England
Piermont Public Library	Piermont, New Hampshire
Arthur and Letty Pounder	Manchester, England
Michael and Stephanie Reed	Alexandria, Virginia
Mark and Clare Rhine	Denver, Colorado
William and Molly Romer	Martha's Vineyard, MA.
Bob and Karin Salome	Laconia, New Hampshire
Nancy Spears	Bristol, New Hampshire
Will Truitt	Bridgewater, NH
Linda Vollmerding	Laconia, New Hampshire
Philip and Diane Wells	Laconia, New Hampshire
Geoffrey and Anne Wilkinson	Chadderton, Lancs. UK
Roger C. Woodberry	Moultonboro, NH

Edwards Brothers Malloy
Thorofare, NJ USA
June 17, 2013